TRAIL RIDING

The Wilderness from Horseback

This book is dedicated to the
Trail Riders of the Canadian Rockies

ACKNOWLEDGEMENTS

My thanks to the many people who have helped in some way with this book by proofreading, checking facts and in general putting up with my one-track mind between the time I thought of writing, on an airplane to Calgary, to the time the camera-ready copy was sent to the printer, over a year later. Special thanks to my daughter, Lesley Dylan, for her careful attention to details of grammar, spelling and the choice of words, my daughter-in-law, Wendy James, who helped with details of horsemanship, and Jerry Fortis who printed my black and white photographs. I shall ever be grateful to my husband, Arthur, who although he never rides, encouraged me to finish this project.

WARNING — DISCLAIMER

The purpose of this manual is to educate and entertain. The author and Plas y Bryn Press shall have neither liability nor responsibility to any person or entity with respect to any injury, loss or damage caused or alleged to have been caused directly or indirectly by the information contained in this book. Every effort has been made to make this book as complete and accurate as possible. However, there may be mistakes, both typographical and in content. Therefore, this text should be used only as a general guide and not as an ultimate source of information.

TRAIL RIDING

THE WILDERNESS FROM HORSEBACK

by

HELEN JAMES

Published by
PLAS Y BRYN PRESS
West Hill, Ontario

Canadian Cataloguing in Publication Data

James, Helen, 1929-
   Trail Riding

Bibliography: p.
Includes index.
ISBN 0-921310-04-8 (bound) ISBN 0-921310-05-6 (pbk)

1. Trail riding   2. Trail riding — Directories.
I. Title

SF309.28.J35 1989   798.2'3   C88-095354-3

All photographs and diagrams by the author unless otherwise indicated.

Printed and bound in Hong Kong
by Book Art Inc., Toronto

Published in Canada by Plas y Bryn Press
Box 97, West Hill, Ontario, M1E 4R4

Preface

This book is about the wilderness and how to enjoy it from horseback. It will help you understand what is involved in recreational trail riding, from choosing a guiding outfitter to mounting a horse and staying on him.

I am talking primarily to the first-time trail rider, the person who has never been on a horse for more than an hour or two. Nevertheless, it's my hope that the person who rides, but who has never been trail riding, will benefit from the experience I have put on these pages.

At first I thought myself audacious to consider writing this book, for I am not, in my own mind — and I'm sure all the guides I've ridden with will agree — I'm not a horsewoman. I have never owned a horse and I don't intend to.

As a child I rode with my family occasionally. I remember a day ride near Lake Louise in Banff National Park, also a mule ride down one side of the Grand Canyon and up the other side the next day, and a donkey ride in Mexico, memorable for the fun we had trying to catch the fleas on my father.

Since then I have been on many rides. My seat may not have improved but I have learned by watching and listening to guides, horse owners, and other riders.

When I speak in this book of my horse or your horse, I am really speaking about the horses an outfitter has allowed us to ride.

My horse is the means of reaching places not otherwise accessible to me. Through trail riding I have been able to explore, wonder at, marvel and rejoice in as well as photograph quiet valleys, rocky peaks, alpine meadows, glacier-fed streams, shelf lakes, snow-covered passes, alpenglow in the sky and glacier lilies at my feet.

They say the best travel books are written by non-natives. If this be so, perhaps a book on trail riding by a non-horse person can make horsesense. You, the reader, will judge.

Helen James

My father believed no child was too young to benefit from travel, so my brother and I went everywhere he did, including down the Grand Canyon. My mother follows Brian, on the pinto mule, and me.

Grand Canyon National Park. Photograph by Col. A.E. Powell.

Contents

My brother, Brian, aged six, obligingly posed for my father on the
Visor atop Half Dome, nearly four thousand feet above the valley
floor. At eight I was wise enough not to. We had ridden horses to
reach the back face where there is a cable attached to the granite by
which climbers can pull themselves up the last eight hundred feet.
My mother had ridden that far with us, but refused the cable climb.

Yosemite National Park, Photograph by Col. A.E. Powell.

1   What is Trail Riding ?

Trail riding is your doorway to the wilderness. This marvellous continent of ours, from the desert at the bottom of the Grand Canyon to the summits of the Rocky Mountains, is accessible by horseback, not only to the young and strong, but to virtually everyone. Five-year olds and ninety-year olds, male and female, fit and soft, the horse makes it possible for all of them to experience the grandeur and the detail of places most people think available only to the hardy backpacker.

Trail riding is riding a horse on a trail as opposed to riding in a ring or corral. When you rent a horse for an hour or two or take your own horse and ride through the forest or along the riverbank, you are trail riding. The more adventurous may ride a horse for a few hours or a few days to get to some scenic area. Thanks to the outfitter's horses in Yosemite my brother and I, then aged six and eight, were able to ride from the floor of Yosemite Valley in California to the south side of Half Dome where there was a wire cable to help us climb to the summit.

Trail riding for more than one day can involve camping, as with the Trail Riders of the Canadian Rockies (TRCR), who establish what might be called a base camp in a different scenic area each summer. The rides last for six days; each day the riders lunch at a different point of interest. In the afternoon they return to their teepees in time for dinner. The TRCR, from its inception in 1923 until 1942, had one moving camp ride each year. When this became too large for safety, the smaller fixed camp rides were initiated. It was not until 1983 that small moving camp rides were reintroduced. Fifteen people, including Bunny Robinson—who had been on that last moving ride back in 1942—and the writer, rode for sixteen days from the Town of Banff to the Town of Jasper, a distance of 240 miles. Since then the TRCR has offered a number of moving camp—now called Safari Expedition—rides each summer, most lasting six to eight days.

Ron Warner, of Holiday on Horseback in Banff, and Ron Moore, of Skyline Trail Rides in Jasper, offer a number of moving camp rides of various lengths, some having lay-over days. Wherever you decide to trail ride there will be guiding outfitters ready to help you. Chapter 11, "Finding an Outfitter," contains a list to help you find many places for such an adventure.

Trail riding may involve sitting in a saddle for a number of hours every day. Saddles, if they fit the rider, are comfortable, and most people do not find this a problem. The exertion is less than hiking and it's the horse who is getting his feet wet and muddy. Your guide will stop every couple of hours so everyone can dismount, stretch his legs and have a smoke.

The horses you will ride should be gentle and co-operative. Ill-mannered horses have no place on the trail and most outfitters will use them as pack animals or get rid of them. Some outfitters breed their own horses for temperament, stamina and intelligence. The Montana Travler has been specially bred for trail riding, but quarter horses, Appaloosas, Morgans, Tennessee walkers and various other breeds and crosses can all make good trail mounts. Trail horses have a good sense of balance. You need not fear they will fall on a steep trail. Even when one foot slips they still have three left to steady them. When you first mount, if you are not used to riding, you will seem high in the air. Sometime during the first few hours you will get accustomed to the height and think no more of it except to appreciate the better view. Also, I find I can see much more of the scenery when mounted than on foot because I don't have to watch where I put my feet. The horse is doing that for me.

Your outfitter will provide the horses, saddles, tents and food. You are responsible for providing a sleeping bag and clothing. Details about what to take can be found in Chapter 3.

Food is always good and plentiful. Cowboys work hard—their working day is usually longer than yours—so they need nourishing food. Very few food items will be dried; ninety percent will be fresh.

Encounters with bears are few—I've never even seen a bear while on a trail ride or in camp. In the wilderness bears fear humans and will keep their distance. If a bear is nearby, your horse will likely sense it long before you see it, so you are not likely to be surprised. Where there is a fixed camp and bears might be a problem an electric fence will discourage them completely.

This book is concerned with recreational trail riding and is primarily written for the person who will sign up with an outfitter in order to see the desert, the valleys, the mountains or other fascinating features on this earth. In this book I refer to horses, but everything said about horses can also be said about mules. Mules make excellent animals on the trail, both for riding and packing. A mule can carry one third more weight than the same size horse while eating one quarter less food. Mules are said to be more stubborn than horses; perhaps this is because they are more intelligent. They can also be more patient. Mule or horse makes little difference if you have a good saddle and your mount has been well trained.

Packing, that is, loading a pack animal and securing the load, is another subject. I recommend the little book *Horses, Hitches and Rocky Trails, the Packers Bible* by Joe Black, published by Johnson Books, Boulder, Colorado, now in its 23rd printing.

Besides recreational trail riding, there is competitive trail riding. I have come across three distinct forms. Some trail riding groups judge the participants on horsemanship while on the trail. Other groups organize what I call "hitchhiking races" where two people share one horse, one riding and one running. The rider hitches the horse and runs ahead. When the runner reaches the horse he rides it ahead and hitches it, and so on. The third type of competitive trail riding is endurance racing. In these grueling matches, man and horse cover as much as one hundred miles in a day. The riders wear track shoes so they can run up the hills to spare their mounts, which are frequently checked by a veterinarian who can disqualify them if there are signs of exhaustion.

There is something in trail riding for everyone. Non-competitive sightseers like me find recreational trail riding provides an ideal outdoor holiday. Some people get so hooked on the experience they return to the mountains or desert every year.

Trail riding is climbing, climbing, up the valley, across the scree and then through a notch in the sheer rock face to the top and over the pass, dotted with mountain avens.

South Molar Pass, Banff National Park.

Trail riding is standing at the summit, exhilarated by the mountain air, excited by the effort and awed by the view.

Guide Dennis Orr, South Molar Pass, Banff National Park.

Trail riding is wending your way along the bank of a glacier-fed river, following the packhorses carrying all the gear and food you will need for a week's journey. The proud palomino Caballo follows willingly when left free, but will lie in the trail when tied in the pack string.

Pipestone River, Banff National Park.

Trail riding offers vistas seen only by backpackers and riders, we
thought, until we came across tracks left by mountain pedal bikes
on this rocky summit.

Allenby Pass, Banff National Park.

Trail riding is crossing rivers. Follow the leader so your horse won't accidentally step in a hole. Sometimes it isn't funny to take an unexpected swim, though everyone laughs when it's someone else.

Brazeau River, bordering Jasper National Park.

Trail riding is hot dusty trails. A kerchief can be used to rinse the
grime from your face in the next icy brook.

Near the Red Deer River, Banff National Park.

Trail riding is meeting old friends and spending days and evenings together, talking of times gone by and to come. No telephone, no doorbells, no city pollution. Connie Turner and Faye Geary, their homes now half a continent apart, renew their friendship while sharing their mutual love of horses.

Near the Red Deer River, Banff National Park.

Trail riding can take you up, into, and across the snows...

...where, in the saddle of a pass, a surprise awaits. A tiny sapphire pond reflecting the snowy peaks. A few seconds after this photograph was taken a young member of our party threw a snowball into the water, destroying the reflection. Another photographer, who was still climbing to a higher vantage point for his picture, was still muttering twenty minutes later.

Maligne Pass, Jasper National Park.

Trail riding is sleeping under the stars or in a tent—if you're lucky,
a teepee with a wood stove in the center.

Teepee Town on the Panther River, Banff National Park.

Trail riding can take you across buttercup carpets.

Near Palliser Pass, Banff National Park.

For me, trail riding means rising early and catching an ice-rimmed reflection of the dawn sky.

Coral Creek, wilderness area south of Jasper National Park.

2 Who Trail Rides ?

Some people trail ride the first time for the adventure, the scenery, the people; some because they like horses. They return for all these reasons and more. I trail ride because, for me, it is the best way to get into the mountains away from the crowds. Our national parks are crowded close to the highways and quiet away from them. On horseback I can easily be twenty miles from a road within a day, and if I'm on a moving camp ride, I can travel up valleys, cross mountain passes, to explore regions seen by few.

Friendships made on the trail last forever. When the trail ride is over we scatter to far away places; when we meet again the friendships rekindle.

It is not necessary to be an athlete to trail ride. Many people trail ride even though they are not fit—either because of their lifestyle or through some disability. It would be more accurate to say these people trail ride because of their problems rather than in spite of them. My horse carries the load my back won't and his feet keep the weight off my fallen arches.

The one underlying reason people trail ride is their need to touch the wilderness. When we smell the pine gum, breathe the ozone under a waterfall, spot an elk grazing above the tree line, see wildflowers in their natural habitat and abundance, watch a zillion diamonds light the night sky, we give our life perspective and regenerate our beliefs.

The riding ability of trail riders varies from the rank beginner to the expert who has ridden all his life, owns his own horse, and rides every day. A good guiding outfitter will take this into account and match the horse to the rider. The expert may be given the spirited young horse, who, although willing, needs to learn a few manners; the beginner or young child will be given an easygoing horse, patient through experience and age.

Do not overestimate your riding ability. Cowboys have a wry sense of humor. I remember one young dude who, although strong and fit, knew not a whit about riding. On the third day as I watched this unfortunate soul jounce on his jackhammer trotting horse I mentioned quietly to one of the cowboys this young man might be more comfortable on a horse with a slower gait, or perhaps we could teach him to post. The cowboy replied, "He told us he was an 'expert,' so I don't reckon we could do anything."

Trail riders I have met include factory workers and judges, snowplow operators and diplomats. . . . Their occupations would fill a book. A human's need to experience the wilderness has little to do with his everyday job.

Trail rider Dr. Bruce Hatfield, co-author of *Matters of Life & Death,* published by Wood Lake Books, tells of a gentleman who arrived at the trail head for a six-day ride with nothing but the clothes he was wearing. Suitable clothes and a sleeping bag were rounded up from other riders for his use. Several days later, when he asked someone to take an instant picture of him so he could prove he had been there, it came out that he was a resident of a nursing home two thousand miles away. He knew he would be thwarted in his plan to trail ride and therefore he had signed himself out for the afternoon suitably dressed to visit his daughter. Instead he took the bus to the airport.

According to his abilities and his needs each trail rider will gain something different from the experience. Originally I went back to trail riding to show my children the mountains. Now, when I go on a ride it is to experience the mountains, re-experience spring, which comes much later above the tree line than in Southern Ontario, where I live, and to use my camera. But, that is not all. I go to meet again some of the riders from other years, and to meet new people. And now I go to show my granddaughter the mountains, the alpine meadows, the glacier-fed streams, the shelf lakes, with the alpenglow in the sky and the glacier lilies at our feet.

Warm clothes and rain gear are essential on all mountain trail rides. The first week in July an unexpected blizzard arrives at lunchtime. It is short-lived, but chilling. Our guide, Gord Thomson, with snow in his hat brim, lights a huge warming fire while others make coffee.

Johnston Creek, Banff National Park.

3   What to Take

An outfitter will greatly appreciate your efforts to keep the weight of your duffel down to thirty pounds or less, depending, of course, on the length of your trip. Everything you take will be transported by pack animal, so, no trunks, suitcases or other containers difficult to pack on a horse, please. The best container is a duffel bag, that is, a bag made of canvas or cordura nylon shaped like a large sausage. An old army duffel bag packs on a horse easily, but it is difficult to find what you need in it without unpacking the whole thing, if it opens at one end. I use two smaller duffel bags, 11 inches in diameter and 29 inches long, with full length zippers. When the outfitter insists on only one piece of duffel, I use a larger bag which is 17 inches in diameter and 32 inches long. Inside your duffel everything should be packed in plastic bags to keep it dry in case of rain. Take along extra plastic bags; they always come in handy.

No matter where you ride, you should be prepared for the weather usually expected in that area. You should also be prepared for the coldest and wettest it's ever been, as well as the hottest and driest. You can always not wear that extra sweater or those sunglasses, but you'll be proud of yourself for being well prepared if the weather changes from the normal. You don't have to take your thick down-filled hunting jacket; you can get the same warmth by layering your clothes. I've often started the day wearing long johns, cords, a short-sleeved T-shirt, a long-sleeved shirt, woolen sweater, down shirt and down vest. As the day warms up or we climb down to a lower altitude, I peel off one layer at a time, tying the shed clothes on the front of my saddle.

The most important item is your sleeping bag. It should be more than adequate for the conditions you expect. Even in July, in the high country there will be frost regularly and you could run into a freak blizzard—you can always unzip a bag that's too warm. If you don't have a cold-weather sleeping bag use two light-weight bags, one inside the other. Some people claim this is warmer than a winter-weight bag. Do not underestimate the importance of being warm at night. A good sleeping bag can make the difference between a successful and exciting adventure and an absolutely miserable trip.

Under your sleeping bag you need a pad or mattress of some kind, for comfort, of course, but more importantly, to insulate you from the cold ground. Air mattresses work well, but are relatively heavy; foam pads are good but are bulky and get damp; back-packer's sleeping pads are the lightest in weight but provide minimum comfort; a self-inflating air mattress is worth the price if you will use it often. It is warm, comfortable, lightweight, and it rolls compactly. Unless you are certain your outfitter provides tents with waterproof floors you should also take some sort of groundsheet. I always take one anyway, sized about four feet by seven feet. Even if I don't need it under my sleeping pad I use it to "shuffle my duffel" morning and evening.

You should have three sets of clothing, including the one you're wearing, plus extra items important to you. Three pairs of cords; I prefer cords to jeans because they do not suck up water as quickly or stay damp as long and they are more comfortable. Three light-weight shirts, two short-sleeved and one long; one woolen sweater; one down shirt; one down vest; two sets of long underwear, one of which doubles as pajamas. I prefer good old one-piece long johns, made of a wool and cotton blend, with a trap door. They are awkward when nature calls, but I never get cold from gaposis. My second set, the two-piece outfit I use as pajamas, is designed as work clothes for construction men and is 100% polypropylene, which retains its insulating value even when wet, dries extremely quickly and is soft and comfortable. For cold nights I take a loose fitting toque to keep my head warm. Extra socks and underwear take little space. Most people take along a bathing suit, though I use the one I wear all the time.

Smaller items you might need include gloves, handkerchiefs, towel, washcloth and all the other toiletries necessary to make you feel human. This includes a small first-aid kit and your medication and vitamins. Other items too numerous to mention here are listed at the end of this chapter.

For wet weather I use a riding slicker; some people use ponchos or rain suits, but since I trail ride every year where rain is frequent, I splurged on a good slicker which not only keeps me warm and dry from my neck to my ankles, but also keeps my saddle and saddlebags dry. Plastic slickers are inexpensive, but they are prone to rip. The riding slicker I use is a heavy plastic-coated fabric. There are others, preferable—but hard to find—made of rubber-coated fabric which does not stiffen in the cold. Both of these cost four or five times as much as the inexpensive plastic ones. If money is no object, the newly available Australian-type slickers and the English waxed slickers, which cost double what mine did, are as comfortable and as elegant as you can get in the pouring rain.

Cowboy boots are by far the preferred footwear for comfort and safety. The heel will prevent your foot from accidentally going all the way through the stirrup, which can be very dangerous. If you do not wear cowboy boots you should at least wear a shoe or boot with a heel and no decorative buckles that could catch on the stirrup or leathers. You will need rubber covers to go over your cowboy boots. These will keep your feet dry on rainy days and when crossing rivers. You may also wear them in the early morning when the grass is wet with dew. Take along a pair of track shoes or other comfortable footwear to wear around camp, and maybe a pair of hiking boots.

Most experienced riders wear leather chaps to keep their legs warm and dry, and to help prevent scratches when riding through brush.

I wear a felt cowboy hat, hot weather and cold. I've tried straw, but they won't stay on my head in the slightest breeze. My felt hat keeps the sun off my forehead and the rain off my neck. The secret of getting a felt hat to stay on is to wear it all day in the pouring rain, or soak it in a stream, and then jam it on your head and wear it until it is dry and has taken the shape of your head. Just in case, I tie my hat strings to a buttonhole on my shirt on windy days. Should you lose your hat while riding, remember it's an old custom to buy a six-pack for the cowboy who retrieves it.

I've listed in chapter 10 the camera equipment I take, and that always includes two rolls of film for each day of the ride and an extra battery.

If you feel you should have some items with you on the horse, use saddlebags, not a backpack. A backpack will tire you and may upset your balance because it raises your center of gravity. If you're not taking a camera you may be able to carry everything you need for the day in your pockets. My saddlebags are fairly small, made of leather with straps and buckles to close them securely. Some larger bags of plastic-coated fabric are unsatisfactory; they tear and are difficult to keep centered on the saddle. If you are tempted to make saddlebags, as I was, beware of fasteners other than buckles. My unfortunate friend, Terry, for whom I made the saddlebags, watched her camera lenses scatter over an alpine meadow as her horse jogged.

The pros and cons of taking your own tack are discussed in chapter 7. I take my own reins because it is important to me to have them long so I can knot and hang them over the saddle horn as I take photographs.

You will need a flashlight. Candles should be avoided because of the danger of fire. They are forbidden in my tent.

If you are diabetic or hypoglycemic, take along necessary snacks, at least for the first day. Cowboys are prone to eat lunch late. After the first day you'll probably be able to keep a part of your lunch as a mid-morning snack for the next day. Some guides make no special effort to choose a lunch spot near water, so you would be wise to take a small flask.

If you smoke or drink, remember to take your own supply; there will not be a corner store nearby. There is often a "cocktail hour" while dinner is cooking, or you may want a little something in the evening.

If you intend to fish, check with your guide ahead of time so you can obtain a license if one is required. Don't be tempted to fish without a license. Not only will you be embarrassed and possibly fined and risk having your equipment confiscated, your guide could lose his guide's license as well. If you do intend to fish use a rod that separates or telescopes and store it in a rigid container.

Last, but not least, remember to take cash to tip the staff. It is usual on the last day of a trail ride to take up a collection and present it to the lead cowboy, who will

----

divide it among the various cowboys, cooks and whoever else worked to make
your ride a success. I usually donate between two and three percent of
the cost of the ride.

Notes:

THE AUTHOR'S PERSONAL PACKING LIST FOR A SIX-DAY MOUNTAIN TRAIL RIDE

Items not packed in the duffel:

- saddlebags
- riding slicker
- boot covers
- flask, cup, snack
- reins
- hat
- camera, accessories
- knife

Items packed in the duffel or worn:

- 2 duffel bags
- sleeping bag, winter-weight
- mattress, self-inflating
- 3 shirts, 2 short-sleeved, 1 long-sleeved
- down vest
- 2 sets long underwear, 1 used as pajamas
- 10 pairs woolen socks, 5 heavy-weight, 5 light-weight
- towel, soap, and washcloth
- deodorant
- insect repellent
- personal medication
- matches and solid fire starter
- cord for clothesline
- notebook and pen
- topographical map
- cash for tips
- plastic bags
- ground sheet
- 3 pairs of cords
- down shirt
- woolen sweater
- 10 sets underwear
- 2 pairs shoes or boots
- gloves
- 3 kerchiefs
- toque
- toothpaste and brush
- comb
- first-aid kit
- wildflower book
- flashlight
- extra shoelaces
- toilet paper
- compass
- sunscreen

Dr. Bill Campbell shows his son Luke the cutthroat trout he has
landed at Luellen Lake.

Banff National Park.

Horse and rider relax
after descending from
snow-covered Job's
Pass. Tomorrow we
tackle even deeper snow
on Poboktan Pass
*Brazeau River, Jasper National
Park.*

From Johnston Creek we climb way above the tree line and then above the vegetation line to a rocky ridge from which we can look eastward to the Sawback Range.

East of Johnston Creek, Banff National Park.

After tying our mounts in the shade our guide leads the lunch horse down to the grassy shore of Elkhorn Lake where someone has already started the fire for coffee.

Banff National Park.

Alternating layers of soft sandstone and limestone have been worn away by the elements, leaving strange formations where a harder layer has protected the top. With a little imagination you can find Queen Victoria presiding over marching troops and ladies carrying large baskets on their heads.

Bryce Canyon National Park. Photograph by H. C. Dell.

I had not seen Yosemite Valley since the 1930's, so when my husband and I were in California recently I jumped at the chance to revisit an old friend. On the way there I wondered if I would be disappointed. Would this place of my memories be as grand as when I was a child? Yosemite was brighter, bolder, higher, narrower, with more waterfalls than I remembered. As a child I had hiked this trail, (see page 119); now I had a mule to carry me.

Trail to Glacier Point, Nevada Falls in the background, Yosemite National Park.

Occasionally we find ourselves in a place so right for us we never forget it. This pass, covered in lichens and low shrubs, will always haunt me. The first time I saw it was in September on my way from Banff to Jasper when the colors were mellowed by autumn. Our little group stopped here for lunch, drawing water from the tiny rivulet for coffee and tea.

Divide Pass, Banff National Park.

The following June I travelled through the same area in the opposite direction. The plant life is now green with spring. The feeling is different, but still haunting.

Divide Pass, Banff National Park.

The tiny living things in this harsh environment with such a short growing season never cease to fascinate me. Poking out of the lichens was a small puffball, which I consumed for lunch. Later I was horrified at what I had done, but at the time I felt such a unity with this place it seemed natural to make a part of it my own.

Divide Pass, Banff National Park.

Willowherb, related to fireweed, often grows in stoney creek beds.

Banff National Park

Just where the tree line ends and the steep rocky cliff begins there is often a shelf lake, usually not visible until you are upon it. This one delights early visitors with a carpet of glacier lilies nodding their heads on twelve-inch stems.

Back Lake, near Palliser Pass, Banff National Park.

After a hearty lunch with
only one piece of bread—
the other loaf got wet when
the lunch horse fell in the
river—several of us walked
back from the shores of this
lake to the scree we had
crossed on our way here.
Growing in the debris
trapped by the broken stone
and warmed by the summer
sun were tiny nodding
onion, barely four inches
tall, pussytoes, arctic
current, sedum, forget-me-
not, Jacob's ladder, silky
phacelia, columbine and this
showy false hellibore.

Leman Lake, Banff National Park.

Dr. Margaret Churcher stretches out tired muscles after a long day in the saddle. Stretching and relaxing after a day's ride can ease, if not prevent, soreness.

Banff National Park.

4 Fitness and Health

How fit do you have to be to go on a trail ride? The answer is, just as fit as you want to be. The more fit you are, up to a point, the less will be your chance of discomfort from riding. On the other hand, the completely unfit may find the experience unique and so enjoy it more than the fit person who has been in the wilderness canoeing or backpacking. The unfit may never before have thrilled at being on top of the world looking down the mountainside just climbed.

Don't let your lack of physical fitness deter you from trail riding. If there is no time to prepare ahead, either because you are too busy or you've signed up for a trail ride on the spur of the moment, don't despair. Many people soft from city jobs go on trail rides over and over again. You'll have the time of your life.

If you have time, improve your cardiovascular system, strengthen your muscles and increase your flexibility. Find a fitness class at your local Y or community center, or take up walking or jogging or some sport. The important thing is to use your body regularly, two or three times a week, if possible. If you join a fitness session, take note of the stretches. You'll find stretching out those muscles after a day in the saddle will help prevent stiffness. The cowboys claim the best way to avoid soreness from riding is to square dance 'til midnight, and they have a point.

After a long day's ride, when the chores are done, some relaxing physical activity will prevent stiffening. If dancing is not available, a walk will serve the same purpose.

While you are on your horse you can ease soreness by stretching and relaxing your legs. Wait until you're on level ground, your horse is caught up and there are no gaps in the line ahead. Remove your feet from the stirrups, stretch your legs straight, push your toes down, then your heels, rotate your ankles, ride for a while with your feet out of the stirrups, legs relaxed. *Never* lift one foot over your horse's neck. This is so dangerous, you don't want to hear about it. And, don't be shy about asking your guide for a break. If you need one, others probably do also.

Your "sitz" bones, if you're not a frequent rider, will undoubtedly get a little tender, but only a little. If you get really sore there is probably something wrong with your saddle and you should mention it to your guide. Not everyone is the same size or shape and you may be more comfortable on a different saddle. If your knees or "sitz" bones become intolerably sore, as can happen to the most experienced riders on occasion, don't be ashamed to dismount and walk a while. I remember our outfitter, Ron Warner, of Holiday on Horseback, walking several miles north of Scotch Camp in Banff National Park. There is a second reason for walking. Riding does not give the same stimulation to the bowels as walking and you may find it necessary to walk to keep regular.

In 1983 Barbara Rostron and I formulated the theory that "stiffness of the knees while riding is immediately relieved by emptying the bladder." The following year, as I waited at the trailhead for my horse, I rummaged up the courage to say to the guide, "We don't know each other yet, but I suffer from TLB—that's tiny, leaky, bladder—so we're going to stop every ninety minutes on the trail."

Two ladies behind me, also strangers, said in unison, "Oh, good!" As it turned out, the cowboy understood completely; he once had a partner whose limit was twenty minutes. Your guide, I'm sure, will be equally co-operative. Your comfort and enjoyment are his concern, for how else can he secure your return.

Much discomfort can be avoided by dressing properly. Loose clothing, worn in layers, will make it possible for you to adjust to temperature changes during the day. Wear well broken-in jeans or cords. They should not have thick seams down the inside of the leg, nor should they be skintight. Panty hose or long underwear under your jeans can prevent chafing.

Make sure you wear comfortable footwear; unscented talcum powder inside your socks can help keep your feet comfortable.

Mosquitos, black flies and other biting insects seem to be attracted by scents in soap, shaving lotion, deodorants, etc. They also prefer blue and people who have recently eaten bananas.

An allergy to horse dander may not wipe out trail riding if you have the willpower and the cooperation of your doctor and your guide. One trail riding doctor tells of a lady, allergic to horse dander, but keen to trail ride at least once with her friends. She did not go near the corral; the horse was brought upwind for her to mount, and she rode directly behind the guide so the amount of dander she was exposed to would be minimal. She continued her usual medication. Her doctor had provided her with stronger medication in case of emergency, but it was not needed. If you are allergic to horses, consult your doctor before undertaking such a venture. On the other hand, people who ride in the mountains are often delightfully surprised to find their hay fever clears up since the vegetation is different.

Everyone should take along his regular medication and any emergency medication he might need. The guide will probably have some first-aid training, and he should have some medical supplies for emergencies. But, he may not have what you need. He couldn't possibly carry all the medications his riders might require. Personally, I carry my prescription medication, vitamins, Band-Aids, adhesive tape, an antibiotic ointment, and aspirin.

Should a medical emergency arise, your guide will be capable of dealing with it. He may ride to the nearest ranger station or other place with a radio or telephone to summon help. Few places where you will trail ride are more than an hour or two by galloping horse from a radio or telephone. It may have taken you three or four days at a steady walk to get where you are, but your guide knows the quickest route to summon help, and he can ride a lot faster than you can.

Your best insurance against illness or injury on a trail ride is common sense and know-how. Keep your body warm, dry and well-fed, treat your horse with respect, and use tools carefully.

5 Getting on and Getting Along with your Horse

Say "hello" to your horse when your guide first gives you his reins. Talk to him softly and reassuringly, using his name. If you would like to pet him, continue talking and then begin gently by rubbing his neck. Do this slowly with no sudden movements. Outfitters' horses have new riders on their backs every few days and some of these riders are real yahoos. Your horse may have come to distrust every dude until he proves himself. Later, when your horse has come to like you he may let you rub his forehead or gently pull his ears. Take it as a compliment when he shows his trust in you by rubbing his head on your shoulder or back. I always try to show my horse I'm a gentle cooperative being in the hopes he'll follow my example. In this I've seldom been disappointed.

Your cowboy is familiar with your horse and his idiosyncrasies. It is important for you to listen and do as he says regarding your steed, for if it were not important, your guide would not mention it. Cowboys are short on words except when it comes to evening around the campfire when the bear and blizzard stories start to roll.

Many guides will tell you not to let your horse eat. It is not that grazing would be harmful to your steed, but rather that your guide doesn't want the ride to move at a snail's pace as one horse after another stops to munch. A horse has no stomach as such, so his digestive system works best if there is an almost continuous supply of food passing through it. It is not his nature to eat three meals a day as we do. I always allow my horse to eat while waiting, whether I'm on the ground holding his reins or mounted. They all soon learn I'll let them graze as long as it doesn't hold up the line. On several rides I refused to let my horses eat, but I found they all got even with me one way or another, usually by walking over my foot.

If you have saddlebags, put them and your slicker or other rain gear on your saddle. Until you get to know your horse and he gets to know you, it is wise to ask someone to hold your horse's reins while you do this; then you can do the same for someone else. There are two leather thongs hanging from each side of the back of your saddle; thread them through the holes in your saddlebags, then divide them so you can lay your rain gear on top of the saddlebags and tie it on with two bows. If you have other clothing you'd like to carry on the saddle, you can tie it on the front in the same way.

Before you mount, check the cinch—that's the band around the horse's rib cage behind his front legs holding the saddle on. The cinch should be tight enough to prevent the saddle slipping as you mount, but not banjo-string tight. With your hand held flat against the horse's side, you should be able to slip four fingers under the cinch. If it seems loose, have your guide check it. Some horses shrink after they are saddled because they puff themselves up as the saddle is put on. The cinch then gets loose when they relax. You should check the cinch *every* time you are about to mount, even if you have only dismounted for a moment, because your horse may continue to shrink all day long as he digests his food.

When it comes time to mount your trusty steed, stand on his left side. Place one rein on each side of his neck, hold them both in your left hand and shorten them so his head is up and he's alert. Talk to him; then, while facing his rear, grab a hunk of mane or the saddle horn along with the reins in your left hand. While still facing your horse's rear, turn the stirrup with your right hand and put your left toe in it. You're going to be careful not to kick the horse's side with your left foot as it turns when you mount. Give a little jump with your right leg—and a heave with your right hand on the back of the saddle, especially if you're short-legged and heavy like me—and swing your right leg up, over the saddle, being careful not to scrape your horse's rump with your right foot. Sit down gently in the saddle and place your right toe in the stirrup; you should be able to stand on the balls of your feet—not your insteps—in the stirrups.

Your guide will probably adjust the stirrup length for you. If you do it yourself you'll have to dismount. The stirrups on a western saddle cannot be safely adjusted from horseback. You should be able to put your hand under your seat while standing in the saddle, or if you take your feet out of the stirrups, they should hit your ankle bone. Stirrup length is an individual matter and you may like them longer or shorter. As you gain riding experience you will be more comfortable with longer stirrups; short stirrups often feel better to a beginning rider, but they lead to stiff knees.

You may prefer to face your horse while mounting so both his head and his hind quarters are visible. This also avoids the possibility of poking the horse in the ribs with your toe as the stirrup turns around.

The reason for mounting your horse while facing his rear is so that if he should move off, his motion will help you get aboard. If you were facing his head with one foot in the stirrup when he moved off, he could drag you by that foot. While we're talking about bad scenarios, you can avoid being seriously hurt by ensuring nothing attached to your horse is attached to or wrapped around you.

Be especially careful while holding the reins or halter rope that neither loops around any part of your body.

When you're used to mounting and if you are strong and agile, you can hold the reins and mane in your left hand and place your right hand on the saddle horn as you jump up. Don't try this until you are really sure of yourself. You don't want to slip and frighten your horse.

If there is no way you can reach the left stirrup from the ground, the easiest solution is to put your horse in a ditch or on a sidehill and mount him from the uphill side. I find standing on a stump unsatisfactory. My horse always moves away just as I reach for the stirrup, leaving me feeling like the cartoon character with one foot on the dock and the other in a canoe.

If you're still having trouble reaching that left stirrup from the ground, consider your clothing. Tight jeans are fashionable in the city, but you'll notice the working cowboy wears his loose enough to mount his horse easily.

Once you're up on your steed, sit comfortably centered in the saddle. Your horse does not mind carrying you, but he'll find it easier if you're not leaning to one side. A good way to ride is with both reins held in one hand just in front of the saddle horn and the long ends held in the other hand over your thigh. If your horse is grazing when the rest start to move off, don't yank his head up and jab him in the ribs. That is no way to make friends. Talk to your steed, tell him it's time to go now, and carefully raise the reins a little while touching him gently with your heels. Horses are gregarious by nature and they hate to be left behind; yours will move off once he realizes the journey has started, and he'll like you for the respect you've shown him. If he doesn't move off, be a little firmer until you get results. There is no need to be rough, just pull the reins with enough force to get his head up, and then increase the pressure of your heels until he moves. Once you are under way you should be able to feel the bit in the horse's mouth. Since a trail horse will want his head low so he can see where he is stepping, the reins may be long. Nevertheless, you should have very gentle contact with his mouth so you can signal him with the slightest movement of the reins.

Horses have likes and dislikes for other horses as we do for other people. If your steed wants to be close to his best friend, let him unless there is a compelling reason not to. Maybe you'll become friends with his best friend's rider. If your horse is disturbed by another horse or another horse dislikes him, you'd be wise to keep them apart. A horse will show his distaste for the horse behind or beside him by pulling his ears back, giving a dirty look, and perhaps by kicking. If you see the horse in front or beside you lay his ears back, keep yours well away. You do not want to be caught between your horse and a flying hoof. If your horse is the one who kicks he will likely give a little sideway movement with his rear as he takes aim. When you feel this, you can often prevent the kick by distracting him with your voice or a touch with your heels.

While on the trail, head to tail, your horse will willingly follow with no guidance from you. Since there is nowhere for him to go but to follow the tail ahead, there is no need to urge him constantly forward with your heels. In other words, sit back and relax. Let your horse do the work. He knows his job and he's remarkably willing to do it.

Now, I do not mean you should give your horse no instruction. Depending on how he feels about his job, his rider, and the day, he may need more or less guidance. What I am saying is, it's wise to start with gentle signals, repeating them while you talk to him softly until he does as you ask. You do not have to take no for an answer; keep urging him firmly but kindly until you get results.

The rider who gets on a strange horse and immediately and harshly sets out to show who is boss often has a rough ride.

Speaking of signals, let's briefly describe how to start, stop, and steer your horse. To start your horse, carefully raise his head, if it is lowered, by pulling the reins upward and then gently touch him with your heels while you tell him it's time to go. If he doesn't start to move or you want him to go a little faster, squeeze with your legs and nudge him again and again with your heels until he goes the speed you desire. Do this carefully. If you kick him too hard, he may think you want him to take off at a gallop.

To turn your horse, keeping your hand low, move the reins—which you are holding in one hand—to the side you want to go. Western horses move away from pressure, so yours will turn his head away from the rein touching his neck. If he is obstinate and won't turn on this signal, you can tighten one rein only to pull his head around. After you have done this several times, he will come to know you mean business and likely will respond to neck-reining.

To stop your horse, sit back in the saddle, say "whoa" and gently pull the reins back, keeping your hands and your voice low.

A horse's mouth is naturally very tender unless it has been spoiled by heavy-handed riders. You should assume your horse has a sensitive mouth and ride him accordingly. The slightest movement of the reins will convey your message. You can signal a good horse by shortening the reins as little as a quarter of an inch by curling your fingers toward you. While we're talking about reins, remember they are important in controlling your horse. If you should drop one and you cannot reach it safely and quickly, it is often safest to say "whoa" and dismount immediately.

As mentioned before, you should sit straight in the saddle—but that does not mean you should be stiff. Your lower spine should be supple and relaxed; it wiggles back and forth absorbing the horse's movement so your head and shoulders move forward smoothly. You can think of your waist as a shock absorber. It is easier on you and the horse if you move with each other cooperatively.

The three main gaits of a western horse are the walk, jog, and lope. These correspond to the walk, trot and canter in the east. In the beginning, when your horse jogs, the easiest and safest thing to do is to stand on the balls of your feet in the stirrups. Once you are fairly comfortable with standing and you can feel your horse's rhythm, you can gently sit down with every second step he takes. This is called posting. Despite widespread rumors to the contrary—especially in the east—posting is easily done in a western saddle, and your horse will appreciate not having you bounce all over his back like a sack of potatoes. The stirrups on a western saddle are longer than those on an English one and you sit in it rather than on it. The rider's movement while posting tends to be back and forth rather than up and down.

To ride your western horse at a jog without posting, you must learn the western roll. The movement is exactly the same as walking—a relaxed and flexible lower spine wiggling in rhythm with the horse to keep your head level. Depending on your horse, you may have to wiggle very fast. It takes most adults a lot of practice and you'll find it easier on some horses than others.

Try to keep your hands low; you'll have better balance and the low reins will keep your horse's head low. You'll also look neater, especially if you can keep your elbows close to your sides. Only John Wayne looks good flapping his elbows as he gallops into the sunset.

No matter what your horse's gait, walking, jogging, or loping, you should keep your heels pressed down. At first this feels awkward but it will make a better rider of you.

Loping is to be avoided until you're comfortable jogging. You can keep your horse at a jog while he catches up by talking softly to him and shortening the reins a little. The signal to break into a lope is to shorten the reins and then quickly release them as you nudge him firmly with your heels. So, if you shorten the reins, keep your heels away from him or you may gallop off to meet John Wayne.

If your horse does break into a lope—and he's likely to when he sees a long gap in front of him on fairly smooth ground—hang on, sit back, relax and stay centered by squeezing with your legs and keeping your heels pressed down in the stirrups. You'll find it an easier gait than the jog once you get the rhythm. Again, relax your lower spine, letting your belly button wiggle back and forth with each stride your horse takes. Try not to lean forward as this will encourage your horse to go faster.

Never put on or take off clothing—except gloves—while on horseback, even at a standstill. Horses have exceptionally good eyesight which they depend on to keep them out of danger. When they see danger, their first defense is to run. Your horse cannot see behind his head so he will be easily frightened by anything coming quickly into view over his ears, like that poncho you're trying to put on. One poncho caught by a gust of wind over your horse's head can start a stampede. Your guide will agree it's safer to dismount when you want to take off or put on clothing.

There are several things you can do to help your horse on steep hills, both up and down. When your horse is climbing, you should get your weight as far forward as possible. On very steep climbs you can grip with your lower legs while you stand in the stirrups and grab a hunk of mane so your horse can pull you up with his strong neck muscles. When going downhill, you should stick your feet out front to keep you from rolling over his head, and lean back in the saddle. Be sure to give your horse enough rein to see his way down safely. A good trail horse will carefully pick his way down, one foot at a time. He's probably a better judge than you of the best route, so let him choose the way, unless, of course, he decides to go under a low branch that could knock you from the saddle. Under no circumstances should you allow your horse to jog or lope down anything but the gentlest slope. This is an easy way for him to slip and pull a muscle. You could end up walking home leading your lame horse.

While on the trail it is common courtesy and safety to stay behind the guide unless he asks you to do otherwise. While your guide is ahead of you, he is choosing the correct route, and he is your safeguard against a runaway. A wise guide will insist. Our guide, Dennis, on one occasion when two young boys loped past him, made sure they would remember how displeased he was by having them wash all the dishes that night for thirty-five people.

In some areas where the environment is particularly sensitive, such as alpine meadows and tundra, it is important to lessen the impact you and your horse cause. If there is a trail, stay on it; if there is no trail, the horses should scatter, each going his own way, so as not to create one.

When crossing a stream or river, you will notice your guide crosses first to find a safe passage, and then he may station his horse facing you just downstream from his crossing point. Be careful your horse follows your guide's path as closely as possible so he won't accidentally step in a hole and send you swimming. If the river is fast or deep, your horse will have a tendency to wander downstream, which is why your guide has positioned himself where he has. If your feet are in danger of getting wet, you can lift them forward, but *never* double them backwards where your heels might tickle your horse. If you can't keep your feet dry, so be it. Next time wear your rubber boot covers.

You won't want to think about falling off, and it will probably never happen on the trail, but if a fall is inevitable, you should take your feet out of the stirrups and keep your arms close to your body. Avoid sticking your arms out as if to break your fall. You won't break your fall, but you could break a wrist, arm or collarbone. If you roll frontwards over your horse's head, or to one side of it, tuck your head in and do a somersault to land on your upper back. You won't fall very far, maybe three or four feet at the most. Drunk people seldom get hurt when they fall because they are relaxed. If you can go limp as you fall off your horse, you are less likely to be injured.

The only time I have fallen off a horse on the trail was when I remounted after retrieving a plastic bag someone had dropped. It was my own fault, for I failed to check the cinch, and my saddle slipped around dumping me kerplunk on my back as my horse jogged to catch up. My companions could have helped by holding their horses still until I was safely in the saddle.

When it comes time to dismount, tell your horse what's happening and untie the reins if you've knotted them. Hold both reins in your left hand along with the saddle horn, slip your right foot out of the stirrup, stand on the ball of your left foot and swing your right leg high over your horse's rear. Before your right foot touches the ground, remove your left foot from the stirrup and slide down your horse's side on your belly, holding the saddle horn with your left hand and the cantle—that's the rise at the back of the saddle—with your right. You don't want to be caught with that left foot still in the stirrup if your horse decides to move off again. If your horse does start to move off while your left foot is still in the stirrup, climb back into the saddle immediately and stop him again before dismounting. Once safely on the ground, put the right rein over his head and hang on to your horse until your guide tells you what to do or takes your horse from you.

Do not tie your horse for the first time until you have checked with your guide. Some horses will not be tied, though they are otherwise gentle and obedient. Wally, an experienced trail rider, did not know the black horse, Alice, would not be tied. Unfortunately, as she pulled back to show her displeasure, the halter shank wrapped around Wally's fingers, resulting in serious injury. Thanks to the fine stitching of Barbara Rostron, one of three doctors on that ride, the wounds healed well and no permanent damage was done. But we all learned a lesson.

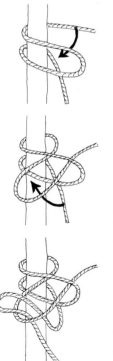

If your guide tells you to tie your horse, choose a strong live tree. When a tied horse pulls back on a dead tree or branch that breaks, there are fireworks.

If your horse has a halter as well as a bridle, have the guide show you how he'd like the reins tied up, or let them hang on the ground while you tie him with the halter rope. Otherwise tie him with the reins. Tie him short and tie him high, as high as his ears if you can. I like to use the highwayman's hitch or a quick-release knot because when I want to untie my horse, I simply pull the end and the whole knot falls apart. That way there is no possibility of getting the reins looped around me. To do the highwayman's hitch, double one of the reins and pull the loop only around the tree; pull a loop of the rein attached to the horse through loop number one, and then pull a loop of the free end through loop number two. Snug the whole thing, pulling the end attached to the horse to be sure you've got it right. When it comes time to leave, pull the free end and everything undoes itself. Try it with a shoelace or a piece of rope first so you'll get an idea of how it works.

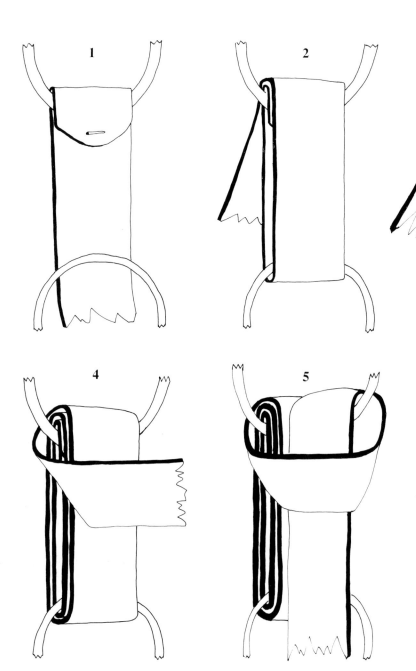

TYING THE FLAT KNOT

1   THREAD THE LATIGO THROUGH THE CINCH RING FROM THE BACK.

2   PULL IT UP AND THREAD IT THROUGH THE D-RING ON THE SADDLE FROM FRONT TO BACK.

3   REPEAT STEPS 1 AND 2.

4   FOLD THE LATIGO FROM LEFT TO RIGHT HORIZONTALLY ACROSS ITSELF.

5   THREAD IT UP THROUGH THE D-RING FROM BACK TO FRONT AND DOWN THROUGH THE HORIZONTAL LOOP FORMED IN STEP 4.

TIGHTEN THE CINCH BY PULLING UP ON THE SECOND LOOP OF THE LATIGO AND THEN SNUG THE KNOT.

6   **More about Horses**

Most horses, like other animals, do not like to have you look them straight in the eye. In animal language it is not only rude to stare, but it is also a sign of aggression. You are less likely to disturb a horse if you avoid direct eye contact and approach him by walking toward his shoulder rather than his head.

When you are near a horse, whether walking past him or adjusting his tack, let him know where you are at all times by talking to him and perhaps by keeping a hand on him. A surprised horse, no matter how calm he may be at other times, will often protect himself from unknown danger by kicking.

When leading your horse by the reins or halter rope, walk well in front of his feet by keeping the reins or halter rope short and your elbow bent so your hand will be close to your shoulder. The idea is to keep his feet well away from yours. To turn him away from you, straighten your arm and push it out sideways so he turns before you do. To turn your horse toward you, lengthen the reins, make the turn yourself and then let him catch up to you before you shorten the reins again. If for some reason you lead your horse with long reins or a long rope, keep well in front and to one side and be alert he doesn't overtake you. Horses will rarely step on people except by accident.

While walking a horse down a steep incline, stay well to one side, whether you are leading him or letting him go on his own with his reins tied up. Ask the guide to show you how to tie the reins around his neck; do *not* hang them over the saddle horn. If the ground is slippery or there is loose gravel be especially careful not to put yourself where the horse could bump you if he should slide.

When holding a horse's rope or reins be careful never to make a loop which could accidentally wrap around you. If they are too long, *fold* them in your hand so they can pull free without wrapping around you. Never coil a rope in your hand if it is attached to a horse.

Occasionally your horse will balk, that is, he will refuse to go where you want him to. He probably sees something strange and until he's convinced it's safe he just won't pass it. You can help him by letting him know you see the suspected danger, so talk to him, shorten the reins a little, and urge him on gently. You may have to reassure him for quite a while before he'll move on. This is why you have been trying to build his trust in you by showing him you're alert, sensible, and gentle. If he has come to trust you he will eventually do as you ask. If you're not at that point yet, dismount and lead him past the offending object.

Sometimes a horse will shy away from people sitting or lying on the ground because he doesn't recognize them as humans. If your steed is anxious about someone on the ground, ask the person to stand up so your horse can see he's a human.

If your horse won't move at all and you don't know why, check his tack. There could be something loose or undone and he is trying to save you from a fall. While starting down a steep trail above the Quinlan Lakes in Banff, my horse not only refused to move, but he did a gentle sideways dance when I urged him forward. As it turned out, his breast strap was undone. This would not have resulted in a fall for me, but I was pleased my horse was concerned for my safety. Once the breast strap was rebuckled, my horse became his usual quiet and obedient self.

Some guides are adamant; only they adjust the tack on their horses. A guide's livelihood depends on keeping his horses fit and well-mannered and yours may feel this is done more easily if he tends everything himself. He may also feel it is safer to let only experienced people tend his horses. If your guide feels this way, respect his wishes and find other ways to be helpful.

If you are comfortable around horses and your guide does not mind, you may be able to help with the chores. Start by unbridling and unsaddling. As you become more accustomed to the tack and your horse, you may want to try putting on the bridle and saddle, but only with your guide's consent.

Do not take the bridle off your horse until you check with your guide. Your horse should be in a corral or you should have a halter with a rope attached. Even if your horse is in a corral it is wise to use a halter. Start by standing on the left side of your horse and put the halter rope around his neck so he'll know you're still in control. You should hold on to the halter rope during the entire unbridling procedure. Examine the bridle carefully so you'll recognize which strap goes where when you go to put it back on. Make a mental note of how much slack there is in the throat and chin straps before you unbuckle them. While holding the halter rope in your right hand slide your left hand up the horse's neck and slip your fingers under the top straps of the bridle, pushing them forward over his ears. As you let the straps down slowly in front of your horse's head he will let go of the bit. Double the reins over the head strap and then hang everything over the saddle horn.

WESTERN SADDLE

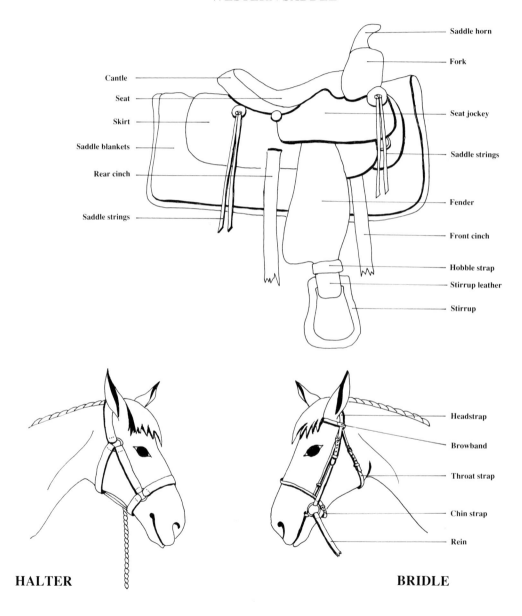

Saddle horn

Fork

Cantle

Seat

Skirt

Saddle blankets

Rear cinch

Seat jockey

Saddle strings

Saddle strings

Fender

Front cinch

Hobble strap

Stirrup leather

Stirrup

Headstrap

Browband

Throat strap

Chin strap

Rein

HALTER

BRIDLE

68

Open up the halter so your horse can put his nose in it. Most horses get to know the routine and they will help, especially if they know oats or pellets are waiting. Lift the headstrap gently over his ears and then do up the throat strap. You should be able to get your fist under the buckled strap. You are still holding the halter rope. If there is a breast strap, unbuckle it from the left side of the saddle and bring it over the seat from right to left so it hangs with the bridle. Divide the two thongs on the front of the saddle and tie them tightly around the bridle and breast strap, using an overhand knot and a bow, just as you tie your shoes.

Some horses are head shy, that is, they are afraid to let anyone raise a hand near their heads. If you do raise a hand near them they will quickly pull their heads up or they will back away. Horses are often head shy because some foolish owner or rider has whipped them. If you show anger or frustration in handling such a horse you will make the problem worse because he associates these emotions in a human with being whipped. You will have to take special care with a head-shy horse and work out ways of bridling and unbridling him without scaring him. He probably won't mind you touching him, he just cannot stand the sight of a hand over his head. Unbridling can be managed by undoing the chin and throat straps gently, keeping your arms low and moving slowly while you talk to him. Stand by his neck. With care you can rub his neck with your right hand, and then, while maintaining contact, slide your hand up to the top of his head from the back where he can't see it. Slip your fingers under the top straps of the bridle and pull it gently and quickly forward over his ears and thus off his head altogether.

To unsaddle your horse, make sure the bridle and breast strap are firmly tied to the saddle as above. Undo the rear cinch, if there is one, and then the front cinch. Pull both of them and the right stirrup over the saddle toward you. Put your left hand under the blankets, as well as the saddle, over your horse's withers[1] and your

---

[1] The withers on a horse correspond to the shoulder blades on a person.

right hand under the blankets and saddle at the center back. Lift the saddle and pull it toward you slowly, being careful nothing flops suddenly to frighten your horse. Saddles are heavy; they can weigh forty pounds, so be prepared for an awkward and heavy load. Put the saddle and blankets over a rail to air.

There are two ways to bridle a horse, with advocates for each. The first method works well with an obedient horse who does not throw his head. Hold the bridle by the headstrap in your left hand the way it will go on his head, letting the reins hang loose. Place your right arm up over your horse's head from behind and reach down between his ears with your hand and grab the headstrap. Lift it up and guide the bit into your horse's mouth with your left hand. Most horses will let the bit into their mouth when they feel it touch their teeth. If your horse will not open his mouth you can put your thumb into the corner, where there are no teeth, to open it, and then gently push the bit in with your fingers. Once your horse has the bit in his mouth you gently put the headstrap all the way up, pulling his ears and the front part of his mane forward under it. Now you buckle the throat strap, with a hand's width of slack, and the chin strap, which you should be able to get two fingers under.

The second method of bridling a horse is best for short people or tall horses. Hold the bridle by the headstrap in your left hand as above. With your right arm reach under your horse's muzzle so your hand is on his right side. With this hand take hold of the bridle about half way down. Lift it over the muzzle while you guide the bit into your horse's mouth with your left hand. Put the headstrap over his head and do up the throat and chin straps as above.

Putting a bridle on a head-shy horse is probably better done by your guide. If you want to do it yourself, watch your guide do it first and then get another person to hold the halter rope while you do it. It is common practise to leave the halter on under the bridle with a head-shy horse. Be gentle but firm and keep talking quietly as you work. Once you attempt to do this you should carry through, if at all possible, because if you quit before the chore is completed, you'll find it doubly difficult next time. However, if your horse is near panic or you are likely to loose your temper you'd be wise to let someone else finish this job. With your guide's permission, if there is no other way to do it, you can keep a horse's head down, while you bridle him, by running the halter rope between his forelegs and then tying it to the saddle horn.

When it comes time to saddle your horse, have someone hold the halter rope or reins for you or tie him to a tree or rail. Most guides like two blankets on a trail horse. Make sure the horse's back and the undersides of the blankets are clean and then gently lift the blankets onto the horse's back, with the front well forward over his withers, then slide them back to lay all the hairs down flat. Prepare the saddle by making sure the right stirrup, breast strap and cinches are over the seat. Lift the saddle by its center, front and rear, and put it over the horse's back, well forward over his withers, as you did the blankets, and then slide it back. With your left hand reach under the front part of the saddle and lift the blankets up over the withers to allow air to circulate and to prevent chafing.

Let the right stirrup down and put the left stirrup up on the saddle horn so you can get at the cinch ring. Reach under the horse's belly and bring the front cinch up through the cinch ring and secure it using the flat knot shown in the diagram. It should be snug enough to hold the saddle while you mount but not so tight it causes damage to the horse's skin. Pull the end of a long latigo through the keeper on the front left of the saddle.

If there is a rear cinch, reach under the horse's belly and bring it up so you can buckle it. The purpose of a rear cinch is to prevent the saddle from tipping forward. If it is to work properly, it should be done up snugly, though not as tightly as the front cinch. Be careful it is forward far enough that it cannot slip back, where it will cause a horse to buck. A loose, hanging rear cinch can catch a horse's rear hoof should he scratch his belly.

Sometimes hobbles are used to limit a horse's travel while allowing him to graze. Hobbles are made of leather—best for the horse not accustomed to wearing them—or metal chain. Most horses are good about standing still while you put the hobbles on, which you do by wrapping them around his front feet from the back and fastening them at the front.

If your horse is round with winter fat or his withers are not prominent, the saddle is likely to slip around as you mount him. You can lessen this by pulling back on the saddle instead of pulling downwards as you mount. Horses with withers like this often have a gentle, slow, and smooth jog. The three black sisters, Alice (who wouldn't be tied), Slipper (whose rider bought her from the outfitter), and my horse, Nancy, were all without withers to speak of. I willingly put up with the inconvenience of jumping on one stirrup or the other to straighten the saddle several times a day because Nancy had such a beautiful jog. She was the only horse I've felt comfortable on doing the western roll.

For those who need more information there are numerous good books on horsemanship available, some of which are noted in the bibliography at the back of this book.

After lunch an alpine meadow makes a soft mattress, especially if you started the day at dawn saddling thirty horses.

Banff National Park.

Father and son demonstrate the fine art of packing. Note the straight-sided pack boxes which stand away from the horse's side to avoid chafing. Our guide, Dennis Orr, claims you can judge an outfitter by the simplicity of his pack boxes. Once the load is secure it will be covered with a tarp held in place with a diamond hitch.

Banff National Park.

This mule had the largest head and the kindest expression of any pack animal I've seen. I wonder what goes on behind those eyes.

Whiterabbit Creek, wilderness area north of Banff National Park.

While on my knees photographing small wildflowers I spotted these
arctic current blossoms, invisible from a standing position. My knees
are always dirty and my feet often wet when wildflowers tempt me to
get down to their level.

Leman Lake, Banff National Park.

A friend of George Edgelow, who had planned to come on this trail ride, but found he would not live long enough, had asked George to find a beautiful place in the mountains for him to rest. He chose the shore of iridescent Leman Lake to say a few words in his friend's honor before scattering his ashes. The other trail riders each piled a stone on a large boulder to commemorate the day.

Banff National Park.

Our pack animals are strung out in front of us, their loads covered in faded tarps blending with the muted autumn colors of Rocky Mountain foliage in the fall.

Near the Bare Mountains, Banff National Park.

A side trip in a long journey brought us to a turquoise lake from which our coffee was brewed. Before we had finished lunch, rain created rings in the water and we donned slickers.

Sawback Lake, Banff National Park.

Dr. Bill Campbell fishes for cutthroat trout during our long
lunch break.

Luellen Lake, Banff National Park.

Horse and rider, Tom McBeath, look equally weary after fifteen days on the trail. Tom was seventy-eight when I took this picture in 1983 and he is still trail riding.

Shovel Pass, Jasper National Park.

Our horses splash across Johnston Creek as they return from grazing
early in the morning.

Banff National Park.

High above the tree line, our guide, Dennis Orr, stretched his arm out to indicate four elk resting on the knoll in front of us. Not a sound came from our riders, even the children were enthralled and silent. As we came closer, the four sentinels rose and, slowly, from the dip between them and us, came the whole herd.
We were privileged to see several very young elk. The elders usually keep the babies many miles from humans.

North of the Red Deer River, Banff National Park.

A mule ride down the Grand Canyon takes the rider through all the climatic zones from pine forest found in Ontario, Canada, to desert as in Mexico. My father's color photographs of our family's ride along this trail were lost in a fire and I have not been there since he took the black and white photograph on page 6.

Grand Canyon National Park. Photograph by H. C. Dell.

7 If You Own a Horse

Not all horses are suited to trail riding. The well-cared for animal who spends his time in a stall except when he is ridden in a ring could be unnerved by a mountain trail, not to mention being low horse in the bunch. On the other hand, if your horse is well-used to riding local trails and gets on well with strange horses, you could consider taking him, if your outfitter guide agrees. You probably won't save any money by the time you transport him. Many people I have ridden with own and ride their own horses, but they don't take them on mountain trail rides, although I have one friend who did the opposite. Elaine fell in love with, bought, and took home Slipper, the outfitter's horse she was riding.

The musculature and know-how to negotiate steep rocky trails are not gained in a pasture. I don't know if horses suffer from altitude sickness as some humans do, although it seems logical they might. I would be loath to subject my horse, if I owned one, to that possibility. Horses probably do need time to acclimatize to an altitude change before they are asked to work.

Trail riding over territory similar to that your horse is familiar with would be another matter. There are horse owners' organizations that arrange trail rides in nearby state or provincial parks or similar areas. These can be a lot of fun and since all the horses are new to each other there will be no established hierarchy to disturb yours.

If you decide not to take your horse, you might like to take some of your tack. You could take your saddle, provided the outfitter is willing and it will fit one of his horses. If you have had your saddle made to fit you, as did Curtis, the Hawaiian wrestler I once rode with, it may be necessary for you to take it. Outfitters do not generally keep saddles to carry such huge people.

Another item to consider, one which I take, is a set of reins. Outfitters' reins sometimes are not long enough for me to knot and hang over the saddle horn when using my camera.

If you intend to trail ride on your own without a professional guide, I suggest you ride several times with a guide or group who know the ropes before you go out on your own. The outfitters who give courses on horse packing are noted in chapter 11. Your list of things to take will be greatly expanded from the items mentioned in chapter 3. The little book *Horses Hitches and Rocky Trails,* by Joe Black, mentioned before, will prove invaluable.

8 Making Camp

Some outfitters will do everything, so all you have to do after a day's ride is unpack your duffel; others expect the riders to put up the tents and help with chores necessary for the evening meal.

No matter what, the horses come first. A good guide will unload his pack animals and unsaddle the riding horses immediately and see they are fed.

Second comes the cook tent, if there is one. A good camp cook will, within ninety minutes, provide a full course meal; meat, potatoes, a vegetable, salad, hot biscuits, tea, coffee and perhaps even a freshly made cheesecake—all on a folding woodstove. I always ask if I can help peel potatoes or whatever. When the group works from a base camp, taking daily rides to points of interest and returning for supper—as the Trail Riders of the Canadian Rockies do—the cooks will have dinner ready when you return and there may not be a chance to help prepare the meal; however, help with the dishes is always appreciated.

Your campsite will, in all likelihood, be chosen by your guide, however if you are choosing it yourself be certain you do not set up camp in a flat area near a river or creek which might be covered in water should there be a sudden flash flood.

When putting up your own tent, choose a level spot, if you can find one, and place the door away from the wind if it is cold or raining, towards the wind if it is hot and you need the breeze, or perhaps you should think of having the door face the rising sun. No one method of orienting a tent will suit everyone; you should decide which way will please you. Lay out your groundsheet, mattress, and sleeping bag, and locate your pajamas, toque, and flashlight before it gets dark. Put your sleeping bag stuff sack inside your sleeping bag. At bed time you can put your down jacket or vest in it to use as a pillow. Keep your duffel in the tent to protect it from the dew, rain or animals.

Keep the campsite neat and clean. If your tent uses pegs, put them down flush with the ground or mark them with stones so you won't stub your toes. When you leave your campsite after one night or a week there should be no sign you've been there except your footprints and the firepit. All tins, foil, glass, and plastic should be packed out; paper should be burned and human waste buried.

If you are staying one night and there are not many in your group, recent thinking is to leave human waste on the surface of the ground to rot, covering it with leaves only, for aesthetic reasons, and place any paper in a plastic bag to be burned at the next opportunity. If you are staying longer, or there are many people in your group, you will want to dig a latrine and cover it before you leave.

Some plastic is burnable, but the fumes often contain cyanide so you should be careful not to breathe the smoke. Better you should pack it out.

No matter where you are, you are being watched—by the ranger, the next camper, or your conscience. If possible, take out more refuse than you take in, especially if you come across discarded glass that could injure an animal or cause a fire. Many forest fires have been started by the sun shining through a piece of

---

glass. Things like apple cores and potato peelings can be scattered to rot, but in some areas orange peel is not considered bio-degradable and must be packed out. There is disagreement about firepits. Some insist the ashes be buried and the stones scattered; others think it wiser to leave the firepit for the next camper so the impact will be confined to one place.

When you are about to leave your campsite, take another last look around to be sure you've left nothing behind. The campsite should be left the way you would like to have found it.

Amie Kiddle is happy and secure riding on the back of Dennis Orr's saddle above the Quinlan Lakes.

Banff National Park.

$\mathcal{9}$ Trail Riding with Children

Some six-year olds I've seen had a marvelous experience, enjoying every moment on the trail and in camp, and I've seen older children downright miserable on the same ride.

Little Amie, at six, the youngest child riding with us in the Rockies, was a delight. She rode Pawnee, a dunn quarter horse, halter-led by our guide Dennis. Nothing bothered her until we began our descent from a lookout point above the Quinlan Lakes. On such steep trails you must push your feet firmly forward and lean back lest you roll over your horse's neck. As Pawnee started picking his way down Amie exclaimed, "I don't want to ride down there, I might fall over Pawnee's head!" "It's alright," Dennis assured her, "You can climb up behind me and sit on the back of my saddle."

Amie, once planted behind Dennis with her arms firmly around his waist, announced loudly to one and all, "This is the second safest place to be on a trail ride." "Really," asked Dennis, "and where is the first safest place?" "In bed."

Little Amie had never been on a horse before, nevertheless she had a thoroughly good time and I'm sure she will treasure her memories of that holiday forever.

The important thing Amie brought with her was a sunny disposition and self-confidence. Her lack of previous riding experience mattered not at all. Other children will enjoy trail riding more if they have some riding experience beforehand to give them confidence.

When my two youngest children, aged ten and sixteen, learned I planned to take them on a trail ride in the Rockies, they insisted we should all take riding lessons. This we did, and I'm sure that trail ride in 1975 worked out as well as it did partly because of those few lessons. I hadn't been on a horse myself in thirty years—maybe that's why my children persuaded me to take the lessons with them.

It isn't necessarily the most outgoing child who will be the happiest on the trail. Some active and confident children will master the riding skills necessary in the first day or two, and then become bored with the whole thing and create havoc by galloping their horses over rough terrain and indulging in other high jinks dangerous to man and beast.

A clever guide can channel this energy in useful ways. One twelve-year old I rode with helped jingle[1] the horses every morning at seven. He was as proud as punch, the cowboys welcomed the help and the chief guide knew some of this young man's rambunctious energy had been consumed before breakfast.

But you should not depend on your guide to control your child's energy or ability to create mischief. If he has the wisdom and the time to help your children, marvelous, but that is not part of his job. You are responsible for your children. Insist on behavior that will not annoy nor pose a danger to themselves, other riders or the horses.

_____

[1] Jingle—to ride around a group of grazing horses to prevent them from straying.

Most children are naturally athletic and have no trouble learning the riding skills needed on the trail. As a parent or guardian you should insist your youngster respect his horse as a hardworking animal always willing to please, if he is able, and if he can understand what is wanted of him. Most guides will take time to give basic instruction to a beginner, child or adult. If your child's horse, or yours for that matter, won't do as he is asked, the fault is probably with the rider who has not learned to communicate his instructions so the horse understands. Increasing the strength of the signal is seldom the answer. Gentle firmness, not roughness, will get the message across. If not, ask a competent rider how to give your horse the right signals or reread chapters 5 and 6. If you are inexperienced you may be confusing your horse by giving him two conflicting signals at once.

Some outfitters will provide ponies for young children and this can work well, however, your child may be insulted by being put on a tiny animal. He may do better on a small horse who won't have to jog constantly to keep up.

If your youngster can't mount by himself, you can help by holding his horse's reins while you kneel on your left knee, keeping your right foot flat on the ground to make a step of your knee. You should be facing the horse's rear. Your child can then place his right foot on your knee and reach the stirrup with his left foot.

An inexperienced child may have his horse led by the halter rope by an experienced rider. The reins are knotted and hung over the saddle horn. If your child's reins are knotted be sure to tell him to hold the reins only by the free ends to avoid pinched fingers between the knot and the saddle horn should the horse lower his head quickly.

The child who enjoys a trail ride will appreciate the whole experience. Trail riding in itself can be boring unless the rider also notices and enjoys the surroundings. Interest your children in nature. You, yourself, should learn the geographical features of the area, the terrain, the climate and the natural history, so you can share this information with your child. Teach your child how to read a map so he can keep track of his whereabouts. Buy him a compass and show him how to use it. Help your child to identify trees and flowers, insects and animals. A child can be bored silly sitting in a saddle several hours at a time if his only interest has been television. Children find plants and animals fascinating if they are introduced to the joys of observing. Most of us do not give children credit; we think hobbies like bird watching are for adults only. Not so. Many avid bird watchers started before they became teenagers. A good bird book and a wildflower book will be a joy to you and your children for years. Some even come with special durable covers meant to be carried in backpacks or saddlebags. There are wildflower coloring books for younger children. You could take such a book along on your trip and suggest your child color the flowers he has seen.

Children can take their own cameras—see the chapter on photography. If your child is so inclined, take along his diary; if he has not kept a journal before, this might be a good time to begin.

If there is more than one child on the ride they will usually entertain each other. Don't put a complete damper on them, but do warn them to be careful of rough games, like football, on uneven ground. The only person I know who had to fly out in a helicopter because of an injury was Dorothy, whose leg was broken in a game of touch football.

Make sure your young one is dressed in layers, so he can add or remove layers as the temperature changes during the day. Rainwear is essential and must be carried on the saddle at all times. Small children often have less body fat, they certainly have less body mass, and therefore they chill more easily than adults.

Your child may need one or more layers of clothing sooner than you do when the temperature is falling.

Hats are necessary to prevent sunburn and heat stroke, and in the cool weather to prevent chilling. The brim should keep the sun off your child's forehead and cover the tops of his ears. At high altitudes the ultraviolet rays can burn a child dreadfully if his head is not protected. Your boy or girl will probably be happy to wear a cowboy hat. The style of these hats has been developed specifically to protect the wearer from the sun and to drain the rain away from his neck. Some parents have their young children wear protective helmets, which is a good idea. Your youngster might be pleased to wear a helmet if he knew beforehand the outriders in the chuck wagon races at the Calgary Stampede wear such headgear.

Take along nutritious snacks for your children to keep their spirits up. A hungry child is a cranky child. With the extra activity on a trail ride your child may need to eat more frequently and larger amounts than he does at home. There is also the possibility that lunch will be delayed on the trail, so a wise parent will keep emergency food in his saddlebag.

Let an adult tie your child's horse. Horses must be tied high. Explain to your boy or girl that it is dangerous to tie a horse lower than four feet above the ground and safer yet to tie him as high as his ears. Horses can be seriously injured if they accidentally step over the rope tying them.

While we are talking safety, make certain your child knows how dangerous it can be to tie or loop anything attached to the horse around any part of his body.

With a little planning beforehand you can make your child's first trail ride an exciting adventure he will remember the rest of his life.

There are lots of camp activities to interest and keep your children busy. Don McLean teaches my granddaughter, Melanie Siewert, to chop wood. The safety secret is to keep those legs far apart.

Teepee Town, Johnston Creek, Banff National Park.

Guyed poles hold up the perimeter of the Sundance Lodge before the long center poles are pushed in to hold up the doughnut-shaped roof. A skirt will be draped around the outer poles, enclosing a space for singsongs, socializing, and square dancing, with a warming fire in the middle.

Teepee Town on the Red Deer River, Banff National Park.

Bunny Robinson, a trail rider since 1942 and life member of the Trail Riders of the Canadian Rockies, decorates all the teepees for the TRCR with original designs. She tells me that the drawings are her own, but each tent is painted in the spirit of North American Indian teepees, with a top area representing the heavens, a center motif, and a base depicting the earth.
Teepee Town on the Panther River, Banff National Park.

We've had seven strenuous days on the trail, with nine more to go, when September catches up to us as we make camp. Our guides silently go about the business of cutting poles for the tents and gathering wood for the cookstove and a warming bonfire, the sounds of the saw and axe muffled by the blanket of wet snow still falling.

Whiterabbit Creek, wilderness area north of Banff National Park.

Our campsite appears as chaos, though much is happening. Barbara Rostron is helping Wally change the dressing on his injured hand, saddle-tired muscles are being stretched out, needed coffee is being consumed and ...

... Mark A.D. Reynolds, author of *Hut Cuisine,* a book on back-country cooking, and our cook on this trip, is preparing dinner. Some of the food boxes are lined with styrofoam to keep the meat frozen and other perishables cool. For dinner tonight we will have meat, potatoes, carrots, salad and a freshly-made cheesecake. Good, fresh food keeps the guides as well as the guests well-nourished and in good spirits.

Scotch Camp, Banff National Park.

Even when camp is moved every day, there will be hot water for a
quick wash. Dr. Bruce Hatfield balances a basin on one log and
himself on another. Not the usual hygenic surroundings he is used to,
but washing in the crisp mountain air has its appeal.

Ram River, wilderness area north of Banff National Park.

In Teepee Town a washstand is provided, with ample hot water and mirrors. Simon is one of those people I envy who always looks neat and clean whether in the city or on a trail ride, whereas I always look like I just came out of the mountains, even when I'm in the city.

Red Deer River, Banff National Park

A herd of mountain sheep overcame their natural distrust of humans
to invade our camp in search of much-needed minerals. So desperate
were they that the coals of our fire, which we had doused with
dishwater, were consumed.

Panther River, Banff National Park.

Chores must be done, rain, snow or sun. Pat Wilson, past president of the TRCR, enjoys warming her hands in the dishwater after a cold night. For some of us this was our unexpected first experience at winter camping.

Whiterabbit Creek, wilderness area north of Banff National Park.

Alessandra Herbert, safety helmet in hand, patiently waits for an adult to help her tie Pawnee high so he cannot injure himself by stepping over his reins. Older horses often like children and make an effort to be gentle with them.

Banff National Park.

My granddaughter, Melanie Siewert, and friend, Pam Gledhill, enjoy a quiet moment. We can use the natural fascination most teenagers have for horses to introduce our children to the joys of wilderness travel and the value of physical activity which trail riding provides.

Elkhorn Lake, Banff National Park.

Everyone should have several serene and restful places in their memories. A small, shallow, mud-bottomed pond, unnamed on my topographical map, but the cowboys call it Elkhorn Lake, no doubt referring to the stack of antlers nearby. Each time I come I rinse the trail dust off in the cool water, here seen reflecting the Bare Mountains.

Elkhorn Lake, south of the Red Deer River, Banff National Park.

10   Photography & Trail Riding

If you have a camera, by all means take it on your trail ride, be it a simple pocket model or a sophisticated single-lens reflex. You'll enjoy your memories more and you'll be able to share them with your friends if you have photographs.

Inexperienced riders should keep their cameras in their saddlebags until they are comfortable with their horses and can anticipate their moves. Your horse is most likely to jog to catch up just as you aim your camera. The least that can happen will be a blurred photo of the sky. Other possibilities are a camera bruise on your cheekbone, or you could lose your balance and dismount unceremoniously.

There are a lot of interesting pictures to take. You can start at dawn with the sun coming over the mountain tops, the cook preparing breakfast, the horses being saddled, and then everyone mounting up. At noon you can picture your new friends, the horses grazing, the coffee boiling, and if there is time, you can take a hike or climb to a lookout for more photographic opportunities.

When the day's ride is over you can capture the horses being unsaddled, and all the activities around camp until sunset. The best photographs will be those you take in the morning and evening when the low angle of the sun adds texture.

Keep your camera with you on overcast days. The non-directional light on a completely overcast day will give you excellent photographs of wildflowers and people without the need of flash to get rid of dark shadows. When you keep your camera with you, you'll be ready for happy accidents. Keep your eyes open. As your guide climbs up the trail in front of you he may suddenly appear at the summit as a silhouette against the sky. What a picture!

If you are riding a well-trained horse, and you are accustomed to him, you may be able to anticipate his moves, then if you're secure enough in the saddle to do two things at once you'll be able to keep your camera on a wide strap around your neck or in a special belt pack. If you use a neck strap, make a loop about the size of your waist from one inch wide sewing elastic, or use an elasticized belt with the buckle at the back. Put this around your waist and then lift it in the front and hook it over your camera to hold it steady against your body. The camera neck strap should be shortened so your camera won't hit the saddle horn. The elastic strap or belt will prevent your camera from flying around as you mount your horse or jog. It's a simple matter of pulling the elastic off your camera when you want to take a picture. There are special harnesses you can purchase to hold a camera firmly against you, but most have clasps; I find it easier to use elastic.

When you do want to take that picture from horseback, remember your first concern must remain your horse. Be sure he is alert but calm and the horses nearby are also calm. Tie a knot in the reins, and hang them over the saddle horn, but be watchful and ready to pick them up to control your horse. It will be no problem taking a picture from a standing horse, but be wary, your standing horse will move off immediately if the horse next to him moves. With practice you can also take excellent photographs from your moving horse. Be sure he is close to the one in front and there are no gaps in the line ahead, so he's not likely to surprise you by jogging to catch up. Relax your lower spine so it absorbs the horse's movements and your upper body moves as little as possible. If your camera is light-weight you can take your picture using one hand, leaving the other free to steady you or pick up the reins to control your horse.

The scenery on both sides of you and the string of horses in front are easy subjects, but be careful all your pictures are not of horses' asses. Once you are comfortable with your horse and you can anticipate his moves, you will be able to twist around in the saddle to catch the line of horses and riders following. If you're not comfortable turning around in your saddle, look for opportunities to photograph horses coming toward you as they make a turn. This can be particularly effective if you climb or descend a hillside in a series of switchbacks. Ride at different places in the line to vary your pictures, and ride up front sometimes so you can see any wildlife before it is frightened away.

Because a fast shutter speed is advisable to get a sharp picture from a moving horse, many people use a fast film—that is, one with a high ASA number, like ASA 400. Others, and I am one of them, stick to Kodachrome 25 because it still gives the best color. In general, the lower the ASA rating of a film the better will be the color rendition and the less grainy the image will be. When using a slower film like Kodachrome 25 or 64 you can still use a fairly fast shutter speed— depending on your subject and the day. When photographing scenery from horseback with K25 on a sunny day I use f8 at 1/125 second or f5.6 at 1/250 second. The results suit my purposes. If I focus on something 20 to 30 feet away, the mountains in the background may be a little soft, but that adds to the mood in my picture. If I'm photographing riders I may use f4 at 1/500 second.

If I want greater depth of field[1] I use my 28 mm wide-angle lens. The wider the lens angle the greater the depth of field.

---

[1]The depth of field is the distance between the closest and farthest things in your picture in focus.

Of course, if you have an automatic camera you won't have to worry about all this, or will you? Well, you should if there are any adjustments you can make. If you can, be certain the shutter speed is as you want when photographing from horseback. That is, set your automatic camera to shutter speed priority and let the f-stop look after itself.

What photographic equipment should you take on the trail ride? In general, you should take as little as possible to get the kind of pictures you want. An instamatic with extra batteries does many people well. Others take several of everything. Remember, every item you take will have to be carried on your horse and cared for, sunshine or rain. Take as little as possible and nothing you are not familiar with using. This is no time to use a new camera.

Personally I take:

- camera body with neck and waist straps
- 50 mm lens with hood
- 70 to 150 mm zoom lens
- 28 mm lens
- reversing ring
- neutral density filter
- extra battery
- +3 diopter (close-up filter)
- 2 rolls of film for each day of the ride

With this equipment I can photograph everything from a tiny blossom on the tundra to the distant mountain peaks. My single-lens reflex (SLR) is really too delicate for the rough handling it receives on a trail ride, but I stick with it because I like its light weight. I treat the expense of overhauling it as part of the ride.

I rarely take a tripod or unipod because they are awkward to carry on horseback and cowboys tend to hate them. There are many ways you can steady your camera without a tripod; lean it against a tree or rock, or lie on the ground making a triangle of your arms. A light-weight chain can be attached to your camera so when you keep one foot on the chain you can pull your camera up to steady it. If you do take a tripod, make it a small one and roll it up inside your sleeping bag. I put my extra lenses in clean woolen socks in my saddlebag, being careful to keep the same weight in each side. My saddlebags are fairly small so I can unbuckle them to find whatever I need without dismounting.

With few exceptions my camera stays around my neck; when it rains my slicker goes over it.

If you are flying to your trail ride on a scheduled airline, keep your film away from X-rays. No matter what the airport personnel tell you, all X-rays will affect all unprocessed films to some degree. There are two good ways to avoid X-rays. The best is to buy your film at your destination and mail it to the processor before you go home. When this is not practical, I purchase my films at home and remove them from the boxes and the plastic canisters. I put the films in a clear plastic bag which I carry in my handbag, so the attendant can pass them around the X-ray machine when I ask for a hand inspection. I do the same thing with the exposed film on my way home. I have been told this hand inspection is always granted except in Paris and a few Arab countries—I've never had any trouble.

Photographs, like all art, should tell a story or impart a feeling. The photographer, through the image he creates, communicates to the viewer something of what he feels about the place he is, the objects in the frame, the action he witnesses, the people he sees, and his mood at the time. If there is no communication, the viewer will be bored and say to himself, "Why was that picture taken?"

Before you take a photograph you should ask yourself these questions: Why am I taking this picture? What do I want the viewer to feel about it? If you feel awkward about answering these questions to yourself, make a point of examining a number of good photographs and paintings. Try to analyze what it is about each one that attracts you and see how the artist has conveyed his message.

Let's analyze several of the pictures in this book to illustrate. In the photograph of Alessandra with her horse, Pawnee, on page 106, the message or theme I tried to illustrate was the gentle bond between horse and child. To that end I put myself close to avoid any surrounding or background objects that might confuse or distract the viewer. Child and horse share lowered heads, a relaxed pose and they are loosely joined by the slack reins. The muted colors add to the restful feeling.

The effect I tried to create in the picture of Back Lake on page 125 is one of power and majesty in the rock, water and sky. I hope I have done that by standing back far enough so the size of each element can be appreciated. All elements which could soften the impact, such as wildflowers, people, or trees in the foreground, have been eliminated. Strong light, strong colors, and strong, simple shapes produce impact.

The feeling I wished to impart with the photo of Divide Pass on page 42 was the unity between the humans and the environment even though one is insignificant in size compared to the other. The viewer's eye is lead to the center of interest, the small cluster of people, by the lines of the small creek and the gently rounded hills to either side. The soft shades of the autumn foliage add to the feeling of unity between the people and the place.

Following a few principles of composition will improve most people's photographs. If your photograph has a center of interest it will probably work best if it is **not** in the center of the frame.

Be careful with lines like fences, trails or the horizon. Horizons should be level and should seldom cut your pictures in two equal parts. Most skies are uninteresting, so include only a little sliver of sky or eliminate it entirely, unless, of course, the sky is the subject of your picture. This will force you to aim the camera downwards slightly and you'll get something in the foreground to give your picture a sense of depth. If your center of interest is small, it will help if you have a line to lead the viewer's eye toward it. Diagonal lines and S-curves suggest movement and are dynamic. Horizontal lines are static and can be restful. Beware of lines that lead your eye out of the picture, especially directly out one corner.

Try to avoid lines that coincide. This is called a merger. If two items in the picture merge or an object merges with the frame it confuses or disturbs the viewer. Move around until your subject is separated from other objects and the frame.

When you photograph people or animals be sure they have more room in front of them than behind them, especially if they are moving. Give them someplace to go. Focus on the eyes. When picturing animals or people avoid cutting off an arm or a leg at a joint.

When we see a beautiful scene our eyes dart about, perhaps looking at the texture on the boulder close by, then at the bushes on the near shore of the lake, then the far shore and the trees standing there, up towards the mountain top and back again to the clump of daisies at the foot of the boulder. To get a photograph that will remind us of this place and give us the same feeling, we must be sure to include all those things that have caught our eye. We may have to use a wide-angle lens and a small opening like f16 or f22 so the daisies and mountain tops will be in focus at the same time. Once we are sure we have everything that contributes to the feeling we want in this picture, we have to be sure we don't have anything extra that will detract. That yellow tour bus and the telephone line, the asphalt in the foreground and that pop can will destroy the feeling we have about this place. Move around to avoid what you can, hide the bus behind a clump of trees and put the pop can in your pack to be disposed of later.

Sometimes our eyes focus on a narrower scene. We see only the beautiful fireweed. Our brain ignores the stop sign in the background and that beer bottle in the foreground and also Aunt Mindy's foot in the corner. The color and form of the flowers have attracted us so much we literally do not see all the other things. But the camera does, and so will you when you get your pictures back from the processor. Again, you will have to move around to hide the stop sign behind the trees, wait until Aunt Mindy moves her foot and pick up the beer bottle. You may want to use a large opening, like f4.2 or f2.8 in order to put the background out of focus if it would otherwise detract from the effect you want.

When you look through the lens of your SLR, the opening is as large as it will go, so you are seeing the picture as it will appear if you set the f-stop at its largest. When you press the shutter button, the opening closes down to whatever you have set it at. If you have set it at a small opening, like f22, f16 or f11, the picture you will capture will have much more in focus than you see in the viewfinder, especially in the background. Until a photographer understands this he will often be disappointed with his results. You will not get the picture you see in the camera unless you use the depth-of-field preview or set your opening at its largest.

Choosing a suitable depth of field can be all important. Most scenics should be sharp from front to back. Choose a small lens openings, like f16 or f22, and then put the infinity sign on the scale on your lens opposite the f-stop you are using. This will result in a much larger depth of field than focussing at infinity.

Other subjects, like people or flowers, are often photographed best with the background out of focus. You do this by choosing a large lens opening, like f2.8 or f4.2 and then focussing on your subject. The sharpness of your subject will separate it from the soft background. The background colors will also be muted so they will not intrude as much.

As mentioned before, overcast days can be advantageous to an alert photographer. Colors will be more saturated. You can add more saturation again to colors by under-exposing just a little. You will take some of your best photographs in the magic light that comes with the sunshine following a rain. This magic light will brighten and intensify your colors. Watch for it!

Rainbows and mists can make marvelous photographs, but few seem able to capture them. You will need to under-expose a rainbow in order to intensify the colors, and you should over-expose a mist if you desire to keep a bright airy feeling in the picture.

If you haven't used the f-stop on your camera creatively before, do a few experiments so you will understand the power of this tool. Choose a flower or similar small subject first. Put your camera as close to the subject as it will focus and take the same picture three times, using the largest opening you have (f2.4 or f4.2) to put the background completely out of focus, a medium sized opening (f5.6 or f8) to soften the background, and a small opening (f16 or f22), which will probably give you sharp detail in the background. If your camera has a depth of field preview, use it to check the results. My camera has one, but I never use it because the view I see is not bright enough for my old eyes to see well. Then find a scene with a number of objects, some close up, some far away, and some in between. Take nine pictures of this scene. Focus on a close object and take three pictures, using three different f-stops as above, focus on a middle object and take the same three picture and then focus on a distant object and take three pictures. Write down what you have done so you will know what f-stop produced which picture when you get them back.

This would be a good time to re-read the manual that came with your camera. If the technical side of photography frightens you, just let your automatic camera do its thing and think about the composition of your pictures.

With today's modern light-weight equipment, it should be no problem for at least one person in your party to take photographs. Take lots of pictures; you may never be in this marvelous place again. You will enjoy them for years to come. Photographs will improve your memory, prolonging and intensifying your experience.

It's a long, hot climb to Glacier Point. I remember drinking from the brink of Nevada Falls on the way down and being so thirsty by the time we approached the valley floor that I lay on my belly and plunged my face into the first icy brook I found. This photograph was taken by my father almost fifty years before I returned to take the picture of the same trail on page 41.

Yosemite National Park. Photograph by Col. A.E. Powell.

There is merit in taking black and white photographs. They last. Color photos will fade over the years, as have the slides my father took in the 1930's. They are purple now, but his black and whites are as crisp and clear as when he first printed them.

The author as a child, Banff National Park. Photograph by Col. A.E. Powell.

The mood of a photograph is affected by the content, the lighting and the lens used. A wide-angle lens integrates the elements; mountain tops, pond and cowboy come together.

North of Palliser Pass, Banff National Park.

The misty bridal-veil quality of the waterfall was captured by resting the camera on a boulder and exposing for 1/4 second. By using a neutral density filter to cut down the light, I was able to use a long exposure. With a single-lens reflex camera, the meter will read the reduced light coming through the lens.

Red Deer River, Banff National Park.

The cascades of a large waterfall can be frozen by using a fast shutter speed. The correct exposure for this photograph, taken on a bright sunny day with ASA 25 film, was f16 at 1/30 or its equivalent. I chose f8 at 1/125.

Nevada Falls, Yosemite National Park.

Scenes with deep shade and bright sunlight are always difficult to capture because the range of brightness is beyond the latitude of the film. Our eyes can see detail in both the bright mountains and in the foliage in the shaded foreground. Film cannot do both at once. If the photographer exposes the film for the mountains, the dark area loses detail, if he exposes for the shady area, the mountains and sky will be washed out. Here I exposed for the mountains and depended on the strong shapes rather than detail to give foreground interest.

Devon Lakes, Banff National Park.

Design and simplicity
can make a photograph.
Sometimes the overall
view imparts too much
information, and
isolating a part of the
scene with a long lens
will produce impact
without losing the flavor
of the place.
*Back Lake, Banff National
Park.*

Arnica, a member of the
sunflower family, often
dots the forest floor,
their single blossoms
like drops of sunlight.

Banff National Park.

Cowboys are difficult to photograph because their hats cast dark shadows across their faces. By catching the profile also shaded an interesting silhouette is obtained.

Banff National Park.

Our little group follows the trail left by our pack horses which preceeded us across a barren snow-covered pass. I had never felt so small nor as close to the sky.

Poboktan Pass, Jasper National Park.

Our outfitter and guide, Ron Moore of Skyline Trail Rides, waits for us. We will take a break here, though it is difficult to stretch our legs in the snow. The meter in my camera has given up at this point. I was able to get good photographs because I remembered the exposure on a sunny day is always f16 at 1/ASA or its equivalent, no matter what the subject.

Poboktan Pass, Jasper National Park.

Purple fringe or silky phacelia, one of dozens of varieties of wildflowers growing above Leman Lake.

Banff National Park.

Pulsatilla, a member
of the anemone family,
breaks through the earth
with its large white
blossoms just as the
snow melts. The plant
continues to grow in the
warm sun, carrying the
flowers up to a foot
above the ground.
*Back Lake, Banff National
Park.*

The height a photographer gains by being on horseback often provides opportunities to see reflections on calm days. No polarizing filter is needed to capture a deep blue sky if your camera is pointed northward. None of my pictures in this book was taken with a polarizing filter.

Near the Spray River, Banff National Park.

11 Finding an Outfitter

There are many ways to find an outfitter for your horseback riding holiday. Once you have decided where you would like to ride, you can write to the department of tourism for that area. These addresses are available in the reference section of your public library. For the United States you would look in the *National Directory of State Agencies*. In Canada you'll find the addresses in *Corpus Administrative Index*. All of these departments of tourism will send you road maps and booklets or brochures about attractions in their areas. Some will send you brochures from pack trip organizers in their state or province or a list of dude ranches or stables, some of which may offer pack trips. Those I know about who send out lists of horse pack trip outfitters are Great Britain and Wales, Alberta, Manitoba, Washington, Utah, Michigan, and Montana. If you read the literature from other areas you may find a reference to one or two establishments offering riding holidays. Another source is the *Vacation Directory* put out by the Dude Ranchers' Association, Box 471, LaPorte, Colorado 80535.

While you are at the library you can check the *Directory of Associations*. You will find such groups as the Trail Riders of the Canadian Rockies, the Trail Riders of the Wilderness and various guide's and packer's associations listed. There may be a trail riding group near you. You can also check the magazine section for advertisements in magazines such as the *Western Horseman*. Don't overlook the dude ranches, some of which offer trail rides along with their other attractions. If you have a spouse who doesn't wish to ride he could enjoy the other activities on the ranch while you go on your pack trip into the wilderness.

Personal recommendation is a good way to find an outfitter. Talk it up with your friends; one of them may have first-hand knowledge.

It would be wonderful if I could recommend a large number of places through my own experience. That is not possible, since, being one person with limited time, I can ride with only a small percentage of the outfitters who offer trail rides. Also, management can change from year to year. A place where I rode a number of years ago may or may not offer the same enjoyable holiday today it did then.

Most of the establishments in the list following offer horse pack trips, that is, trail rides involving camping in the wilderness, according to correspondence, brochures, advertisements, and other printed sources available to me. Since there is little wilderness left in Europe, trail rides there are usually horse treks, where the riders stay overnight in local inns. Horse trekking is also available in North America. Outfitters who offer horse treks are identified in the following pages by footnotes. The quality of the services offered by these people may vary greatly, from the primitive to the luxurious. Luxuries are not as important to me as good, well-trained horses and nourishing food. You should investigate for yourself.

The outfitters who offer combination horse pack and river float trips are also identified by footnotes.

Some outfitters (identified by footnotes) offer horse packing schools where participants can learn the art of packing a horse so the load stays put and is comfortable for the horse. I recommend anyone contemplating using their own horses on a trail ride take such a course.

The following list is as complete as possible at the time of writing. Inclusion in this list is not meant to convey endorsement, by the author or the publisher, of any of the services offered by these establishments. This list should be used only as a guide in planning your holiday. No money or other consideration has been accepted from the establishments listed.

There are probably many more establishments who offer horse pack trips, and some of the people listed may have gone out of business recently. The author would appreciate receiving information to make this list more complete and accurate for the next edition of this book.

We have omitted stables who offer only day rides. We have also omitted the names of guides who offer only horse pack trips for the purpose of hunting. It does not seem appropriate in a book designed to help people appreciate and enjoy the wilderness to include information to assist big game hunters.

Outfitters are listed alphabetically under the country, province or state where they operate, although some of them have winter homes in other areas. Where an outfitter or organization works in several areas the address will be listed only once, although the name will be listed under each area, with a reference to help you find the address.

Write to several outfitters in the area you would like to explore, ask for their brochure and mention you found their names in this book. Many are particularly proud of their gentle, surefooted, and well-trained animals, most take pride in the food they offer, all love the wilderness they ride through.

Notes:

AUSTRALIA

Bogong Horseback Adventures
Steve & Kath Baird
Box 230, Mt. Beauty 3699, Victoria

Equitour   See Wyoming

Lovick's Mountain Trail Safaris
Charlie Lovick
Merrijig 3723, Victoria

Macleay Packsaddlers
Bellbrook, via Kempsey
N.S.W. 2400
Phone: 065 67 2040

Stoney's Bluff & Beyond Trail Rides
Graeme Stoney
Box 170, Mansfield 3722, Victoria

Walhalla Mountain Saddle Safaris
Malcolm and Debbie Johnston
Box 26, Erica, Victoria 3825
Phone: 051 65 3365
Telex AA 36597

AUSTRIA
BELIZE

Equitor   See Wyoming

BRITAIN

Equitour[1]   See Wyoming

─────────
[1]Horse trekking

Riding and Trekking Holidays[1]
For information write to:
British Tourist Authority
Thames Tower, Black's Road
London W6 9EL, Great Britain

WALES

For information write to:
**Pony Trekking and Riding Society of
  Wales**[1]
c/o 32 North Parade, Aberystwyth
Dyfed SY23 2NF, Great Britain

Wales Tourist Board
Llandaff, Cardiff CF5 2YZ
Great Britain   022-27281

YHA Adventure Holidays
Trevelyan House, St. Albans, Herts
Great Britain   phone: 55215

CANADA

ALBERTA

Alberta Frontier Guiding & Outfitting
Ed Walker
Box 83, Sundre, Alta T0M 1X0
Bus 403 638-4855   Home 403 638-2897

Alpine Stables Ltd
Box 53, Waterton National Park
Alta T0K 2M0   403 859-2462
Off season: Box 1718, Cardston, Alta
T0K 0K0   403 653-2449

American Wilderness Experience Inc
See Colorado, U.S.A.

Amethyst Lakes Pack Trips Ltd
See Tonquin Valley Amethyst Lakes
  Pack Trips

Anchor D Guiding & Outfitting
Duane or Jan Matthews
Box 656, Black Diamond, Alta T0L 0H0
403 938-2867   403 933-2867

Artindale Guide Service
Doug Artindale
Box 2642, Olds, Alta T0M 1P0
403 335-8532

Athabasca Trail Trips
Box 951, Hinton, Alta T0E 1B0
403 865-7594

Barrier Mountain Outfitters
Box 69, Olds, Alta T0M 1P0
403 556-6778 or 403 556-4053
XJ42733 Sundre Mobile

**Country Corral Guest Ranch &
  Panther Valley Pack Trips**
Amos & Heather Neufeld
R.R. 1, Elnora, Alta T0M 0Y0
403 773-2442   Telex 038-3174

Diamond Hitch Outfitters
Mike and Wendy Judd
Box 2316, Pincher Creek,
Alta T0K 1W0
403 627-2949   403 627-2773

Diamond Jim's Mountain Rides
Jim Colosimo
Box 394, Rocky Mountain House
Alta T0M 1T0
403-845-6859   403 845-6920

Double Diamond Wilderness Trails
John Hatala
R.R. 3, Rimbey, Alta T0C 2J0
403 843-3582 or 403 347-1171

Gladstone Mountain Guest Ranch
Chuck and Val Ridder
Box 2170, Pincher Creek
Alta T0K 1W0   403 627-2244

Griffin Valley Ranch Ltd
Al & Harold Griffin
Box 812, Cochrane, Alta T0L 0W0
403 932-2879   403 932-5869

Guinn Outfitters Ltd
Rick and Denise Guinn
Box 100, Kananaskis Village, Alta
T0L 2H0   403 591-7171   403 275-8066
or 183 Huntwick Way N. E.
Calgary, Alta T2K 4H4

High Country Ride and Fish
Charlie and Margaret Stricker
Box 354, Wildwood, Alta T0E 2M0
403 325-3961

High Country Vacations
Bazil Leonard and Sons
Box 818, Grande Cache, Alta T0E 0Y0
403 827-3246

Holiday on Horseback
Ron Warner
Warner & Mackenzie Guiding &
   Outfitting Ltd
Box 2280, Banff, Alta T0L 0C0
403 762-4551   800-661-8352
Office: Trail Rider Store, 132 Banff Ave

Holmes Outdoor Recreation Ltd.
Ed and Jacqui Holmes
c/o Holmes Mountainaire Lodge
Box 570, Sundre, Alta T0M 1X0
403 637-2229 403 277-5972 or dial '0'
   ask for Calgary Mobile Operator

Homeplace Ranch and Trailride
Mac Makenny
Site 2, Box 6, R.R. 1, Priddis
Alta T0L 1W0   403 931-3245

Horseback Adventures
Tom Jr. and Shawn Vinson
Brule, Alta T0E 0C0   403 865-4777
403 865-2641   403 865-3064
403 866-3746   403 866-3068

J H Trail Rides
Del & Judy Whitford
Box 98, Caroline, Alta T0M 0M0
Until May 20: 403 722-2419

Jasper Wilderness and Tonquin Valley
   Pack Trips
Gord Dixon
Box 550, Jasper, Alta T0E 1E0
403 852-3909

Kananaskis Guest Ranch
Bud and Annette Brewster
Sum: Seebe, Alta T0L 1X0
403 673-3737
Win: Box 964, Banff, Alta. T0L 0C0
403 762-5454

Lost Guide Outfitters
Gary Bracken
R.R. #1, Sundre, Alta T0M 1X0
403 638-4149

McKenzies' Trails West
Ed and Millie McKenzie
Box 971, Rocky Mountain House
Alta T0M 1T0   403 845-6708
403 845-2172   403 845-4018
Base camp : 403 721-2132

Miette Trail Rides and Summer Pack
   Trips
Ed and Margaret Regnier
Box 496, Edson, Alta T0E 0P0
403 723-3380   403 693-2157
Sum: Box 2044, Jasper
Alta T0E 1E0   403 866-2202

Panther Valley Pack Trips
See **Country Corral Guest Ranch**

Rocky Mountain Retreat
Stan A. Radke
Box 641, Red Deer, Alta T4N 5G6
403 340-3971   403 672-9955

Rocky Mountain Vacations[2]
Sundance Mall, 215 Banff Ave.
Box 2319, Banff, Alta T0L 0C0
403 762-4347

Saddle Peak Trail Rides[2]
Dave A. Richards
Box 1463, Cochrane, Alta T0L 0W0
403 932-3299   403 932-7171

Sam Sand's and Son Summer Pack
   Trips and Trailrides
Box 568, Rocky Mountain House
Alta T0M 1T0   403 845-6487
403 845-4190 403 845-6676

------

[2]Combined horse pack trip and
white water rafting also available

Skyline Trail Rides
Ron and Lenore Moore
Win: Brule, Alta T0E 0C0
403 865-4880
July/Aug: Box 207, Jasper
Alta T0E 1E0   403 852-4215

Tilbury Outfitting
Syd Tilbury
Box 366, Grande Cache, Alta T0E 0Y0
403 827-2569

Timberline Tours
Paul Peyto
Box 14, Lake Louise, Alta T0L 1E0
403 522-3743

Timbermountain Packtrain
Dave and Carol Simpson and Sons
Box 511, Claresholm, Alta T0L 0T0
403 625-2931
Win: Box 964, Banff, Alta T0L 0C0
403 762-5454

**Tonquin Valley Amethyst Lakes Pack
   Trips**
Wald and Lavone Olson
Oct-May: Brule, Alta T0E 0C0
403 865-4417
Jun-Sept: Box 508, Jasper Alta T0E 1E0
403 866-3980   403 866-3946
403 865-4417

Trail Riders of the Canadian Rockies
Box 6742, Stn "D", Calgary
Alta T2P 2E6   403 263-6963

Trail Riders of the Wilderness
See District of Columbia, U.S.A.

Ward's Guide & Outfitting
John Ward
Box 717, Jasper, Alta T0E 1E0
403 852-3717

Warner & Mackenzie Outfitting Ltd
See **Holiday on Horseback**

Wild Rose Outfitting
Dave & Rose Manzer
Box 1943, Edson, Alta T0E 0P0
Bus 403 723-4986 Home 403 693-2407

BRITISH COLUMBIA

Beaverfoot Lodge
Box 1560, Golden, B.C. V0A 1H0
604 346-3205   604 346-3216

Chilko Lake Wilderness Ranch Ltd
Box 4750, Williams Lake
B.C. V2G 2V7

Diamond Hitch Guiding and Outfitting
Jim Scott
13120 - 240th St, R.R. 2
Maple Ridge, B.C. V2X 7E7
604 463-8942

Headwaters Outfitting Ltd
Liz Norwell or Brian McKirdy
Box 818, Valemount, B.C. V0E 2Z0
604 566-4718

Mountain Pack Trips
Kari and Paula Leiviska
9550 Spillsbury St, R.R. 3, Maple Ridge
B.C. V2X 8X7   604 462-8914

Leo Ouellet
Box 494, Hope, B.C. V0X 1L0
604 869-9532

Rockhaven Ranch
Pat and Murray Saunders
R.R. #6, 832 Finlayson Arm Rd
Victoria, B.C. V8X 3X2
604 478-3032

Stardust Trail Rides Ltd
Harry and Shirley Schubert
Site 8, Comp 5, R.R. 2, Enderby
B.C. V0E 1V0   604 838-9371

Top of the World Guest Ranch
Box 29, Fort Steele, B.C. V0B 1N0
604 426-6306

MANITOBA

Duck Mountain Outfitters
Leslie E. Nelson
Box 99, Minitonas, Man R0L 1G0
204 525-4405

Milk & Honey Country Trail Rides
Art Hiebert
Box 933, Brandon, Man R7A 5Z9
204 328-7263

Riding Mountain Nature Tours
Daniel Weedon
Box 429, Erickson, Man R0J 0P0
204 636-2968

Trailhead Outfitters
Anne Schuster
Gen. Del., Lake Audy, Man R0J 0Z0
204 848-7649 Winnipeg: 204 775-4743

NEW BRUNSWICK

Broadleaf Farms
Danny and Phyllis Hudson
Hopewell Hill, Albert Cty
N.B. E0A 1Z0   506 882-2349

Norton-Wincroft Stables
Dale & Linda Murray
Norton, N.B. E0J 2N0
506 839-2317

Steeves Mountain Trail Rides Ltd
R R 1, Moncton, N.B. E1C 8J5
506 384-2692

ONTARIO

Christie Beach Farm
R.R. #1, Thornbury, Ont. N0H 2PO
519 599-5082

Graf's Ranch
R.R. #1, L'Amble, Ont. K0L 2L0
613 332-1449

Honora Riding Stable
R.R. #1, Little Current, Ont. P0P 1K0
705 368-2669

Loney's Sportsmans Lodge
Kukagami Lake Road, Box 475, Garson
Ont. P0M 1V0   705 858-1281

Shiner's Stable
Box 26, Cloyne, Ont. K0L 1K0
613 336-8377

QUEBEC

Equitour   See Wyoming

SASKATCHEWAN

Emma Lake Riding Stables
R.R. #1, Christopher Lake,
Sask. S0J 0N0   306 982-4805

YUKON TERRITORY

Ceaser Lake Outfitters
Terry Wilkinson
Box 484, Watson Lake, Yukon Y0A 1C0
403 536-2174

CHINA
COSTA RICA
DOMINICAN
REPUBLIC
EGYPT

Equitour   See Wyoming, U.S.A

FRANCE

Equitour   See Wyoming, U.S.A

Societe Hippique d'Epinal
Ravin d'Olima, 8800 Chantraine Epinal
France

GERMANY
GREECE
HUNGARY
ICELAND

IRELAND
ISRAEL
ITALY
JAMAICA

Equitour   See Wyoming, U.S.A

KENYA

Amber May Safaris
Box 2, Nanyuki, Kenya
Phone: Nanyuki 2193

Equitour   See Wyoming, U.S.A

MEXICO

International Training Programs
University of Oklahoma, 1700 Asp
Norman, OK 73073, U.S.A.
405 325-1941

Lajitas Trading Post
Box 48, Terlingua, TX 79852, U.S.A.
915 364-2234

MOROCCO

WEXAS International
45 Brompton Rd, Knightsbridge
London, SW3 1DE, Great Britain
01-589-0500

Equitour   See Wyoming, U.S.A

NEW ZEALAND

Equitour See Wyoming, U.S.A.

PERU

American Wilderness Experience,
See Colorado, U.S.A.

PORTUGAL

Equitour See Wyoming, U.S.A

SPAIN

Equitour   See Wyoming, U.S.A.

Antonio Figueiredo
13 Macdougal Alley, New York
NY 10011, U.S.A.

WEXAS International
45 Brompton Rd, Knightsbridge
London, SW3 1DE, Great Britain
01-589-0500

UNITED STATES OF AMERICA

ALASKA

Alaskan Adventure
Box 18, Hope, AK 99605

Kachemak Bay Horse Trips
Mairiis Davidson
Box 2004, Homer, AK 99603
907 235-7850

Northland Ranch Resort
Box 2376, Kodiak, AK 99615
907 486-5578 (message)

ARIZONA

Adventure Trails of the West, Inc[3]
Dana W. Burden
Box 1494, Wickenburg, AZ 85358
602 684-3106

American Wilderness Alliance
4260 E. Evans, Denver, CO 80222
303 758-5018

American Wilderness Experience Inc
See Colorado

Carefree Ranch Stables
Larry and Linda Bright
Box 776, Carefree, AZ 85377
602 488-3944

Creder Wilderness Safaris
See Colorado

Grapevine Canyon Ranch
Gerry & Eve Searle
Box 302, Pearce AZ 85625
602 826-3185

Honeymoon Trail Co.
Mel Heaton
Box 4, Moccasin, AZ 86022
602 643-7292

Mountain Shadows Stables & Outfitters
Box 2742, Pinetop, AZ 85935
602 368-5790   602 735-7676

Trail Riders of the Wilderness
See District of Columbia

CALIFORNIA

Agnew Meadows Pack Train
Bob Tanner
Box 395, Mammoth Lakes, CA 93546
619 873-3928   916 926-5794
After Jun 1: 619 934-2345

Alpine Meadows Stables
Box 357, Tahoe City, CA 95730
916 583-3905
Off season: 17172 Bar Paw Place
Grass Valley, CA 95949   916 273-1965

Armstrong Redwoods Pack Station
Box 970, Guerneville, CA 95446
707 887-2939

Balch Park Pack Station[4]
Tim or Diane Shew
Box 852, Springville, CA 93265
209 539 3908 After Jun 1: 209 539-2227

Cedar Grove Pack Station
Tim Loverin
Box 295, Three Rivers, CA 93271
209 561-4621
After May 15: 209 565-3464

----

[3]Horse trekking

----

[4]Packing school also available

Cherry Valley Pack Station
Kay De Voto
Box 5500, Sonora, CA 95370
209 878-3596 After Jun 1: 209 692-5671

Clyde Pack Outfitters
Allen Clyde
12267 E. Paul Ave, Clovis, CA 93612
209 298-7397

Cottonwood Pack Station
Dennis or Kathy Winchester
Star Route 1, Box 81, Independence
 CA 93526   619 878-2015

D & F Pack Station
Brad Myers
Box 156, Lakeshore, CA 93634
415 946-1475
After Jun 15: 209 893-3220

Divide Wilderness Outfitters
See Oregon

**Eastern High Sierra Packers
  Association**
690 N. Main St, Bishop, CA 93514
619 873-8405
Star Route 1, Box 100, Independence
CA 93526   619 878-2207

Elk Creek Pack Station
Box 1158, Happy Camp, CA 96039
916 493-5421

Equitour   See Wyoming

Frontier Pack Train
Dink Getty
Star Rte 33, Box 18, June Lake
CA 93529   619 872-1301
After Jun 1:   619 648-7701

Golden Trout Wilderness Packtrains
Dan Shew
Box 756, Springville, CA 93265
Sum: 209 542-2816 Win: 209 539-2744

Grant Ranch Stables
105 Mt. Hamilton Road, San Jose
CA 95140   408 274-9258

Heart D Guide & Pack Service
Box 517, Ft. Jones, CA 96031
916 468-5548   916 468-2372

High Sierra Pack Station
John or Jenice Cunningham
Sum: Mono Hot Springs, CA 93642
Win: Box 1166, Clovis, CA 93613
209 299-8297   209 532-8297

High Sierra Packers Association
Star Rt. 1, Box 100, Independence
CA 93526   619 878-2207

Horse Corral Pack Station
John or Sandy Vincent
Win: Box 641, Woodlake, CA 93286
209 564-2709
Sum: Box 135 Sequioa National Park
CA 93262   209 565-3445

Kennedy Meadow Pack Trains
Jim & Julie Porter
Box 1300, Weldon, CA 93283
619 378-2232   Win: 818 896-4809

Kennedy Meadows Resort
Willie Ritts
Sum: Star Route Box 1490, Sonora
CA 95370   209 965-3900
Off season: Box 4010, Sonora, CA 95370
209 532-9096

Leavitt Meadows Pack Station
Bart Cranney
Box 124, Bridgeport, CA 93517
916 495-2257

Little Antelope Pack Station
Vic Bergstrom and sons
Box 179, Coleville, CA 96107
916 495-2443 or 702 782-4960

Lor-O Ranch
Sum: Box 915, Cecilville, CA 96081
916 Sawyers Bar Toll Station #4681
Off season: Box 111, Burbank
CA 91503   818 843-1620

Lost Valley Pack Station
Fred or Clara Belle Ross
2410 Mount Pleasant Road
San Jose, CA 95148   408 238-0632

Mama's Llamas, Inc
Box 655, El Dorado, CA 95623
916 622-2566

Mammoth Lakes Pack Outfit
Lou, Mary or Lee Roeser
After Jun 15: Box 61, Mammoth Lakes
CA 93546   619 934-2434 619 934-6161
Off season: Box 198, Coleville
CA 96107   916 495-2312

Mather Pack Station
Joe or Jay Barnes
Sum: Mather, CA 95321
209 379-2334
Off season: 12942 Highway 120
Oakdale, CA 95361   209 847-5753

McGee Creek Pack Station
John or Jennifer Ketcham
After Jun 1: Route 1, Box 162
Mammoth Lakes, CA 93546
619 935-4324
Nov-May: Star Route 1, Box 100
Independence, CA 93526   619 878-2207

Minarets Pack Station[5]
Bruce Negri
Box 545, Dos Palos, CA 93620
209 392-3121
 or 8648 E. Shaw, Clovis, CA 93612
209 299-3929

Mineral King Pack Station
Don Bedell
Box 61, Three Rivers, CA 93271
209 561-4142
After Jun 15: 209 561-3404

Modoc Wildlife Adventures
Box 1882, Alturas, CA 96101
916 233-3777

**Mountain Base Camp Ltd Gold Lake
  Stable**
Route 1, Box 710, N., Quincy, CA 95971
916 836-2491

Mt. Whitney Pack Trains
Box 1514, Bishop, CA 93514

Muir Trail Ranch
Adeline Smith
Sum, Box 176, Lakeshore, CA 93634
Off Season: Box 269, Ahwahnee
CA 93601   209 966-3195

Onion Valley Pack Trains
See **Rainbow Pack Outfit**

Pine Creek Pack Trains[6]
Brian or Danica Berner
Box 968, Bishop, CA 93514
619 387-2797

Rainbow Pack Outfit[6]
Mark Berry
Box 1791, Bishop, CA 93514
619 873-8877

Rainbow Ridge Ranch
Box 1079, Mt. Shasta, CA 96067
916 926-5794

Red's Meadow Pack Train
See **Agnew Meadows Pack Train**

**Reno Sardella's Pack Station, Kerrick
  Corral**
Reno Sardella
Box 154, or Box 495, Jamestown
CA 95327
209 984-5727 or 209 984-5452
Sum: Box 1435, Pinecrest, CA 95364
209 965-3402

Rock Creek Pack Station[6]
Rock Creek Wild Mustang Rides
Herb & Craig London or Dave Dohnel
Box 248, Bishop, CA 93514
619 935-4493 Oct to Jun: 619 872-8331

Schober Pack Station
N. F. Walt and Art Schober
Route 2, Box 179, Bishop, CA 93514
619 387-2343
After Jun 15: Rte 1, Box 4, Bishop
CA 93514   619 873-4785

Shasta Llamas
Box 1137, Mt. Shasta, CA 96067
916 926-3959

Six-Pak Packers
Box 301, Weaverville, CA 96039
916 623-6314

Sky Ridge Ranch
22400 Skyline Blvd, Box 9, La Honda
CA 94020   415 948-8398

Skywood Stables
Rancho Canada Verde
2700 Purisima Creek Rd, Half Moon
Bay, CA 94109   415 726-5188

Spanish Creek Stable
Route 1, Box 710, Quincy, CA 95971
916 283-2290

**Sugarpine Ranch-Crystal Basin
  Outfitters**
Sum: Box 733, Shingle Springs
CA 95682
Off season: 3898 Missouri Flat Rd
Placerville, CA 95667
916 622-4108

Sunset Corral
2901 Vineyard Road, Novato, CA 94947
415 897-8212

Trinity Pack Trains
Box 277, Trinity, CA 96091
916 266-3305

Trinity Trail Rides
Mark & Ruth Hartman
Coffee Creek Ranch
Star Route 2, Box 4940, Trinity Center
CA 96091   916 266-3343

Virginia Lakes Pack Outfit
Tom & Martha Roberts
HC Route 1, Box 1076, Bridgeport
CA 93517   702 867-2591
Sum: 619 932-7767   619 872-0271

Western Pacific Outfitters Inc
9720 Wilshire Blvd, Los Angeles
CA 90212-2094   213 859-1507

Wilderness Outfitting and Guide
   Service
15031 Quartz Valley Road, Ft. Jones
CA 99032   916 468-5349

Wolverton Pack Station
See **Horse Corral Pack Station**

Yosemite Park and Curry Co.
Yosemite Reservations, High Sierra Desk
5410 E. Home Ave, Fresno, CA 93727
209 252-3013
or Dean Conway
Valley Stables, Yosemite, CA 95389
209 372-1248

COLORADO

Adam's Lodge
Robert E. Hilkey
Box 213, Meeker, CO 81641
303 878-4440   303 878-4312

AJ Brink Outfitters
Jim Brink
3406 Sweetwater Rd, Gypsua, CO 81637
303 524-9301   303 524-9510

Altenburg Brothers Outfitting
Eugene K. Altenburg
1333 Emery St, Longmont, CO 80501
 303 772-8428   303 440-0704

American Wilderness Experience Inc
Box 1486, Boulder, CO 80306
303 444-2632

Astradle a Saddle
Gary Bramwell
Box 1216, Pagosa Springs, CO 81147
303 731-5076

C & R Stables & Outfitters
Ray Miller
Box 40221, Silver Creek, CO 80446
800 526-0590   303 887-2131

Capitol Peak Outfitters, Inc
Steve Rieser
17893 Hwy 82, Carbondale, CO 81623
303 963-0211

Cache Creek Outfitters
Jim DeKam
Box 609, Parachute, CO 81635
303 285-7346

Dean Chambers
198 County Rd 54, Meeker, CO 81641
303 878-4473

Clearwater Outfitting
Barry Holtz
Box 4133, Estes Park, CO 80517
303 586-8300

Colorado High Guide Service, Inc
Dennis A. Bergstad
1759 S. Ironton, Aurora, CO 80012
303 751-9274

Cottonwood Cove Lodge
Wagon Wheel Gap, CO 81154
303 658-2242

Coulter Lake Guest Ranch, Inc
C. Norman Benzinger
Box 906, Rifle, CO 81650
303 625-1473

Creder' Wilderness Safaris
28481 State Hwy 160, Durango
CO 81301   303 247-2533
Win: Box 742, Apache Junction
AZ 85220
 602 986-0751 or 602 969-7361

Chuck Davies Guide Service
Chuck Davies
3461 F 3/4 Rd, Clifton, CO 81520
303 464-7421

DTD Outfitters
John D (Jack) Lowe
391 Rodell Dr, Grand Junction
CO 81503   303 243-0837

Delby's Triangle 3 Ranch
Delbert Heid
Box 14, Steamboat Springs, CO 80477
303 879-1257

Double Diamond Outfitters
Jack Wheeler
Box 2, Meredith, CO 81642
303 927-3404

Drowsy Water Ranch
Ken and Randy Sue Fosha
Box 147, Granby, CO 80446
303 725-3456

Elk Mountain Ranch
LaRue and Susan Boyd
Box 910, Buena Vista, CO 81211
Win-Spring: 303 694-2818
Sum-Fall: 303 395-6313

Fossil Ridge Guide Service
Rudy Rudibaugh
711 Ranch Parlin, CO 81239
303 641-0666

Frenchy's Mountain
Bill & Carol Koon
Box 646, Naturita, CO 81422
303 728-3895

The Gunnison Country Guide Service
John C. Nelson
49221 E Hwy 50, Gunnison, CO 81230
303 641-2830

Richard L. Hawkins
Star Rte 305, Howard, CO 81233
303 942-3393

High Lonesome Guide & Outfitter
William A. Hillier
Box 1059, Kremmling, CO 80459
303 724-9685   303 887-3576

Horn Fork Outfitters
Glen Roberts
29178 County Rd. 361, Bueno Vista
CO 81211   303 395-8363

International Adventures Unltd
Michael H. Grosse
Box 1157, Gunnison, CO 81230
303 641-5369

Lazy Double FF Outfitters
Kirk A. Ellison
Freeman's Ranch, Creede, CO 81130
303 6508-2454

Lone Tom Outfitting
Paul Janke
12888 RBC 8, Meeker, CO 81641
303 878-5222

MW Ranch[7]
Bill Diekroeger
19451 - 195th Ave, Hudson, CO 80642
303 536-4206

Mineral Mountain Guide & Outfitter
John Martin
Powderhorn, CO 81243
303 641-2673

Moon Run Outfitters
Doug McLain
Box 401, Snowmass, CO 81654
303 922-4945

Old Glendevey Lodge
Garth W. Peterson
10825 N. Cty Rd 15, Fort Collins
CO 80524   303 568-7396   303 435-5701

Outback Outfitters & Guide Service
Richard Williams
Box 667, Monte Vista, CO 81144
303 852-2038

Over the Hill Outfitters
John R. Neely
3624 Cty Rd 203, Durango, CO 81301
303 247-9289

Dick Pennington Guide Service Ltd
2371 H. Rd, Grand Junction, CO 81505
303 242-6318

Pollard's Ute Lodge
Troy R. Pollard
237 RBC 75, Meeker, CO 81641
303 878-5123

Puma Mountain Outfitters
Roy Best
Box 477, Hayden, CO 81639
303 276-3434

Quaking Aspen Guides & Outfitters
David Mapes
Box 485, Gunnison, CO 81230
303 641-0529

**Rocky Mountain Back Country
Outfitters**
Gerald C. Risner
Box 21, Rand, CO 80473
303 451-6143

Rocky Mountain Outfitters
Jon Dirk Ross
1946 County Rd 333, Ignacio, CO 81137
303 883-2352

Saddletramp Outfitters
Thomas L. Bullock
1531, 335 Rd, New Castle, CO 81647
303 876-2960

Samuelson Outfitters
Richard S. Samuelson
Box 868, Fraser, CO 80442
303 726-8221

Sangre de Cristo Outdoors, Inc
Bill Schulze
Box 586, Westcliffe, CO 81252
303 783-2265 or 303 783-9343

Schmittel Packing & Outfitting
David Schmittel
Box 175, Yampa, CO 80483
303 638-4430

----

[7]Horse trekking

K. E. Schultz Guide Service
Kurt E. Schultz
0010 Ponderosa Dr, Glenwood Springs
CO 81601   303 945-7120

Seven W Guest Ranch
Floyd A. Beard
3412 County Rd 151, Gypsua, CO 81637
303 524-9328

Sid Simpson Guide Service
1148-3950 Dr, Paonia, CO 81428
303 527-3486

Sierra Grande Outfitters
See New Mexico

Six Point Outfitters
Barry Fox
Box 5615, Woodland Park, CO 80866
303 687-6325

Sombrero Ranches, Inc
Rex Ross Walker
3100 Airport Rd, Boulder, CO 80301
303 442-0258

T Lazy 7 Ranch
Rick Deane
Box 858, Aspen, CO 81612
303 925-4614

Taylor Creek Ranch
Vic Taylor
51440 Elk River Rd, Steamboat Springs
CO 80487   303 879-9072

Toneda Outfitters
Ed R. Wiseman
Box 336, Moffat, CO 81143
303 256-4866

Trail Riders of the Wilderness
See District of Columbia

Tumbling River Ranch
Jim & Mary Dale Gordon
Grant, CO 80448   303 838-5981

Twin Pines Outfitting
Larry Darien .
2880 County Rd 3, Marble, CO 81623
303 963-1220

Ultimate Escapes, Ltd
Gary Ziegler
M-115 S. 25th St, Colorado Springs
CO 80904   800 992-4343   303 578-8383

Valley View Guest Ranch
Ray Pyle
Box 528, Lake City, CO 81235
303 944-2284

Vickers Enterprises, Inc
Larry Vickers
Box 96, Lake City, CO 81235
303 944-2249

Vista Verde Ranch
Frank and Winton Brophy
Box 465, Steamboat Springs, CO 80477
303 879-3858

Wapita Outfitter & Guides
Jon Garfall
Box 932, Gunnison, CO 81230
303 641-2603

Weminuche Wilderness Adventures
17754 County Rd 501
Bayfield, CO 81122

Wetherill Ranch
George G. Hughes
Box 370, Creede, CO 81120
303 658-2253

Western Adventures
Harland J. Hauser
1576 S. Badger Ln, Willowbrook, Dillon
CO 80435   303 468-6172

Whistling Acres Ranch
Jerry L. Price
Box 88, Paonia, CO 81248
303 527-4560

White River Resort
Jack Harrison
21679 E. Otero Pl, Aurora, CO 80016
303 690-6627

Wild Horse Outfitters
Harry Landers
1819 Cty Rd 329, Ignacio, CO 81137
303 883-2356

Wilderness Adventure, Inc
Box 82, South Fork, CO 81154
303 873-5331

DISTRICT OF COLUMBIA

Trail Riders of the Wilderness
Office only: Box 2000, Washington
DC 20013 800-368-5748 202 667-3300
1319 -18th St NW, Washington
DC 20036

HAWAII

Ironwood Outfitters
Box 832, Kamuela, HI 96743
808 885-4941

Equitour See Wyoming

IDAHO

Allison Ranch, Inc
Harold & Phyllis Thomas
7259 Cascade Dr, Boise, ID 83704
208 376-5270

American Wilderness Experience Inc
See Colorado

Anderson Outfitting
Bob & Mary Anderson
4990 Valenty Rd, Pocatello, ID 83202
Day: 208 237-6544 Night: 208 237-2664

A. W. Angell
Rte 1, Box 202, St. Anthony, ID 83445
208 624-7026

Bear River Outfitters
Marriner & Eileen Jensen
8989 U.S. Hwy 30, Star Rte 1, Box 1450
Montpelier, ID 83254   208 847-0263

Bighorn Outfitters
Curt Thompson
366 Mill Creek Rd, Hamilton, MT 59840
406 961-3736
Mike Hammett
Box 1103, Pinedale, WY 82941
707 966-0165   307 367-6885

Boulder Creek Outfitters Inc
Tim Craig
Box 119, Peck, ID 83545
208 486-6232   208 839-2282

Castle Creek Outfitters
Dick & Shane McAfee
Box 2008, Salmon, ID 83467
208 344-6600

Chamberlain Basin Outfitters, Inc
Ed & Peggy McCallum
Route 1, Box 240, Salmon, ID 83467
208 756-3715

Clearwater Outfitters
Leo and Virginia Crane
4088 Canyon Creek Rd, Orofino
ID 83544   208 476-5971

Diamond D Ranch, Inc
Randy or Tom Demorest
Clayton, ID 83227
Dec 1 - Jun 1: Box 36005, Grosse Point
    Woods, MI 48236   313 821-4975
Randy: 313 247-2436
Tom: 313 773-5850

Dixie Outfitters, Inc
Emmett & Zona Smith
Box 33, Dixie, ID 83525   208 842-2417

Eagle Cap Wilderness Pack Station
See Oregon

Epley's Idaho Outdoor Adventures[8]
Ted and Karen Epley
Box 987, McCall, ID 83638
Idaho only: 800 233-1813
208 634-5173

------

[8]Combined horse pack trip and
white water rafting also available

Five Bears Outfitting
Gary L Peters
1360 N.E. Summerdale Rd, Corvallis
MT 59828   406 961-4778

Fox Creek Pack Station
Richard Clark
Rte 1, Box 541, Victor, ID 83455
208 787-2222

Gillihan's Guide Service
Bob & Cathy Gillihan
850 Jackson Ave, Emmett, ID 83617
208 365-5384   message 208 365-2750
Radio-tele 208 382-4336

The Grunch Bunch Outfitters &
    Guides
Rte. 3, Box 19, Hayden, ID 83835
208 772-3194

Happy Hollow Camps
Martin R. Capps
Star Rte, Box 14, Salmon, ID 83467
208 756-3954

Hole in the Wall Lodge
See Montana

Idaho Wilderness Camps, Inc
Merritt's Saddlery
Garry and Sharon Merritt
Box 1516, Salmon, ID 83467
208 756-2850

Indian Creek Ranch
Jack & Lois Briggs
Route 2, Box 105, North Fork, ID 83466
Phone Salmon Operator for 24F211

Little Wood River Outfitters
Robert and Terri Hennefer
Box 425, Carey, ID 83320
208 823-4414   208 823-4488

Lochsa River Outfitters
Jack & Sherry Nygaard
HC 75, Box 98, Kooskia, ID 83539
208 926-4149   208 926-0851
Win: Rte 2, Box 30, Potlatch
ID 83855   208 875-0620

Lost Lakes Outfitters, Inc
Al Latch
HCR 66, Box 226, Kooskie, ID 83539
208 926-4988

Mackay Bar Corporation[9]
Garn Christensen
3190 Airport Way, Boise, ID 83705
208 344-1881   800 635-5336

Jim McManus
Box 442, Pierce, ID 83546
208 464-2118

Merritt's Saddlery
See **Idaho Wilderness Camps, Inc**

Middle Fork Lodge, Inc
Bob Cole & Nick Stuparich
3815 Rickenbacker, Boise, ID 83705
208 342-7888   208 342-7941

**Moyie River Outfitters/Sweets Guide
   Service**
Stanley A. Sweet
HCR 85, Box 54, Bonners Ferry
ID 83805   208 267-2108

Mystic Saddle Ranch[10]
Jeff Bitton
Jun 1-Nov 15: Box 0, Stanley, ID 83340
208 774-3591
Nov 15-May 31: Box 2624
Hailey, ID 83333   208 788-3055

Oswold's Pack Camp
Ralph Oswold
Box 192, Kamiah, ID 83536

Palisades Creek Ranch
Elvin or Bret Hincks
Box 594, Palisades, ID 83437
208 483-2545

Paradise Outfitters
Rich & Patti Armiger
HCR 11, Box 74, Kamiah, ID 83536
208 935-0859

Primitive Area Float Trips, Inc[10]
Box 585, Salmon, ID 83467
208 756-2319

Stanley Potts Outfitters
Stan Potts
Box 1122, Hailey, ID 83333
208 788-4584

Quarter Circle A Outfitters
Rick Hussey
Star Rte, Iron Creek, Salmon, ID 83467
208 894-2451

Red River Corrals
Archie & Eileen George
Star Rte, Box 18, Elk City, ID 83535
208 842-2228

Renshaw Outfitting
Jim Renshaw
Box 1165, Kamiah, ID 83536
208 935-0726   208 935-2829

Gerald Richie & Son Outfitters[11]
Gerald Richie
Star Rte, Stage 1, Darby, MT 59829
406 349-2499

Rick's College
Larry B. Wickham
198 Administration Building, Rexburg
ID 83440   208 356-1040

River Adventures Ltd[12]
Mark Hinkley & Sam Whitten
Box 518, Riggins, ID 83549
208 628-3952

Robson Outfitters
Dale Robson
Box 44, Felt, ID 83424
208 456-2861

Rugg's Outfitting
Ray Rugg
Rt. 1, Box 50, St. Ignatius, MT 59865
406 745-4160

Salmon Meadows Lodge
Wagon Wheel Corrals
HC 75 Box 3410, New Meadows
ID 83654   208 634-2556   208 634-8462
208 347-2357

---

[9]Combined horse pack trip and
white water rafting also available

[10] Combined horse pack trip and
white water rafting also available

[11]Packing school also available

[12]Combined horse pack trip and
white water rating also available

Salmon River Lodge, Ind [14]
Steve Dixon
Box 348, Jerome, ID 83338
208 324-3553
or Dave Giles
1704 East Main, Salmon, ID 83467
208 756-2646

Sawtooth Wilderness Pack Trips
See **Mystic Saddle Ranch**

Selway-Magruder Outfitters
Don Habel & Sons
Box 135, Corvallis, MT 59828
406 961-4323

Seven Devils Outfitting
Bob Sentier & Dave Stucker
Box 712, Riggins, ID 83549
208 628-3478
Idaho Tele-Radio in Boise: 208 382-4336

Shattuck Creek Ranch & Outfitters
Andre Molsee
Box 165, Elk River, ID 83827
208 826-3284   208 826-3405

Simons Outfitters
Jack W. Simons
84 Mullan Gulch Rd, St. Regis
MT 59866   406 649-2329

South Fork Lodge
Ellen Shaw
Hwy 21, MP 72
Lowman, ID 83637   208 259-3321

St. Joe Hunting & Fishing Camp Inc
Don E. Dixon & Tom Poage
10405 Newport Hwy, Spokane
WA 99218
Don Dixon: 509 467-5971 509 258-4226
Tom Poage: 509 467-5971

Stover's Outfitters
John H. Stover
Box 604, Council, ID 83612
208 253-4352

Sun Valley Wilderness Outfitters
R. J. and Glenda Lewy
Box 303, Sun Valley, ID 83353
208 622-5019

Sweets Guide Service
See **Moyie River Outfitters**

Teton Expeditions, Inc
Glen R. Foster
Box 218, Rigby, ID 83442
208 523-4981   208 523-3872
208 745-6476

Trail Riders of the Wilderness
See District of Columbia

Trapper Creek Outfitters
Tony J. Popp, Jr
Triple T Ranch, Salmon River Air Route
Cascade, ID 83611
Answering service: 208 382-4336

**Triangle C Ranch/Cummings Lake
   Lodge**
Box 810, North Fork, ID 83466
208 865-2424   208 865-2422

Triple O Outfitters
Harlan, Duane & Barbara Opdahl
Box 21, Pierce, ID 83546
208 464-2349   208 464-2761

Wagon Wheel Corrals
See **Salmon Meadows Lodge**

Wally York & Son Inc [13]
W. Travis York
Box 319, Elk City, ID 83525
208 842-2367

Wapiti River Guides [14]
Gary Lane
Sum: Box 1125, Riggins ID 83549
208 628-3523
Win: Box 72, Cove, OR 97824
503 568-4663

Wildlife Outfitters & Guest Ranch [13]
Jack, Shirley and Rick Wimple
992 Pleasant View Dr., Victor
MT 59875   406 642-3262

KENTUCKY

Equitour See Wyoming

MAINE

Equitour See Wyoming

MICHIGAN

Hell Creek Ranch
10866 Cedar Lake Road, Pinckney
MI 48169   313 878-3632

---

[13]School for outfitters also available
[14]Combined horse pack trip and
white water rafting also available

Wolf Lake Ranch
Route 2, Box 2514, Baldwin, MI 49304
616 745-3890

MINNESOTA

B K Ranch
Mark or Linda
Route 1, Nevis, MN 56467
218 652-3540

MONTANA

A Lazy H Outfitters
Al Haas
Box 729, Choteau, MT 59422
406 466-5564

American Wilderness Experience Inc
See Colorado

Jack Atcheson & Sons, Inc.
3210 Ottawa St., Butte, MT 59701
406 782-2382   406 782-3498

B & D Outfitters
Bob Frisk or Paula Anderson
Box 455, Kalispell, MT 59901
406 837-4423   406 755-8247

Bartlett Creek Outfitters
Mike & Peggy Smith
1190 Quinlan Road, Deer Lodge
MT 59722   406 693-2433

Beardsley Outfitting & Guide Service
Tim & Kristy Beardsley
Box 360, Ennis, MT 59729
406 682-7292

Bear Paw Outfitters
Tim & Cindy Bowers
Rt 38, Box 2032, Livingston, MT 59047
406 222-6642

Beartooth Plateau Outfitters
Ronnie L. Wright
Box 1127, Cooke City, MT 59020
or Box 28, Roberts, MT 59070
Oct-May: 406 445-2293
Jun-Sept: 406 838-2328

The Bear's Den Outfitters
Bruce C. Delorey
Box 941, Livingston, MT 59047
406 222-0746

Beyond Yellowstone
Tim & Tom Wilkes
9354 Nash Rd, Bozeman, MT 59715
406 586-9455

Big Horn Outfitters
See Idaho

Big Sky Pack Trips
Merritt G. Pride
Box 15, Stanford, MT 59479
406 566-2486

Bob Marshall Wilderness Ranch
Virgil & Barbara Burns
Seeley Lake, MT 59868   406 754-228fi

Bridger Outfitters
Dave Warwood
15100 Rocky Mtn Rd, Belgrade
MT 59714   406 388-4463

Buckhorn Ranch, Inc
Harry T Workman
Box 84, Eureka, MT 59917
406 889-3762

Buffalo Horn Outfitters
205 Buffalo Horn Creek Rd, Gallatin
Gateway, MT 59730   406 995-4283

Burnt Leather Ranch
Chuck and Shell Reid
McLeod, MT 59052
406 222-6795   406 932-6155

**Castle Creek Outfitters & Guide
  Service**
John D. Graham
Box 1121 Red Lodge, MT 59068
406 446-2735   406 245-3358
or Box 30, Silvergate, MT 59081
406 838-2301

Cayuse Outfitters, Inc
Dr. Larry A. Lahren
Box 1218, Livingston, MT 59047
406 222-3168

Circle Bar Guest Ranch
Sarah Hollatz
Utica, MT 59452   406 423-5454

Circle KBL Outfitters and Guides
Bob and Kathy Lamberson
Box 25, Stevensville, MT 59870
406 777-5969

Circle 8 Ranch
Al & Sally Haas
Box 729, Choteau, MT 59422
406 466-5564

Crazy Mountain Outfitter & Guides
Ray "Slim" Keefer
Box 54, Clyde Park, MT 59018
406 686-4648

Bob Crick High Country Outfitter
Bob and Linda Crick
1142 Pleasent View Drive, Victor
MT 59875   406 642-3233

Curtiss Outfitters[16]
Ron & Patti Curtiss
326 Bench Dr, Kalispell, MT 59901
406 257-6215

Diamond Hitch Outfitters
Bob & Chris McNeill
Polaris, MT 59746   406 683-5494
or 3405 10 Mile Rd, Dillon, MT 59725

Diamond J. Ranch
Mr. and Mrs. Peter Combs
Ennis, MT 59729   406 682-4867

Double Arrow Outfitters
Jack Rich, C.B. Rich
Box 495, Seeley Lake, MT 59868
406 677-2317   406 677-2411

Gary Duffy
Box 863, Corwin Springs, MT 59021
406 848-7268   406 848-7287

Eagle Mountain Outfitters
Larry & Rebecca Larson
Box 1, Ovando, MT 59854
406 793-5618

Elk Creek Outfitters
Bob Miller
663 Vaughn So. Frontage Rd
Great Falls, MT 59404
or R R 5059, Great Falls, MT 59401
406 761-5184

The Elkhorn Guest Ranch
Maria Freeman
Clinton, MT 59825
406 825-3220

Elkhorn Guide Outfitters, Ltd.
See **Hawkins Outfitters**

Elkhorn Outfitter Service
Henry Barron
Box 1339, Townsend, MT 59644
406 266-5625

Elkhorn Ranch
Mr. and Mrs. Ronald Hymas
Gallatin Gateway, MT 59730
406 995-4291   Win: 406 284-6943

Glacier Outfitters
Gary Abbey
East Glacier, MT 59434   406 226-4442
Sep-May: Rt 2, Box 108 Ronan
MT 59864   406 675-2142

Great Divide Guiding & Outfitters[17]
Richard Jackson
Box 325, East Glacier Park, MT 59434
406 338-2108

Great Northern Float Trips[17]
Reno and Deedee Baldwin
Box 278, West Glacier, MT 59936
800 535-0303   406 387-5340

H & H Outfitters
Dave & Becki Harrington
Box 632, Lincoln, MT 59639
406 362-4581

Hawkins Outfitters
Steve J. Hawkins
Wilderness Lodge
Box 187, Eureka, MT 59917
406 296-2642   406 889-3318

Hidden Lake Outfitters
Bob Bovee
Box 1233, Big Timber, MT 59011
406 932-6582

Hole In The Wall Ranch
Frank DeLeo or Jeff & Maria Freeman
Box 8, Alberton, MT 59830
406 728-5203   Mob Unit #1284
406 793-5702

Horse Creek Outfitters
Bruce and Connie Malcolm
Rte. 1, Box 667, Emigrant, MT 59027
406 848-7144

Iron Horse Outfitters
Box 1346, Hamilton, MT 59840
406 821-4474

Jake's Horses Outfitting
Kate & "Jake" Grimm
Box 191, Canyon Route, Gallatin
Gateway, MT 59730   406 995-4630

JJJ Wilderness Ranch
Max and Ann Barker
Box 310, Augusta, MT 59410
406 562-3653

Klick's K Bar L Ranch
"Beyond All Roads"
Nancy Klick
Augusta, MT 59410
406 467-2771   406 264-5806

---

[16]Combined horse pack trip and
white water rafting also available

[17]Combined horse pack trip and
white water rafting also available

Lazy T4 Outfitters
Spence and Kay Trogden
Box 116, Victor, MT 59875
406 642-3586

Lone Mountain Ranch
Bob & Viv Schaap
Box 69, Big Sky, MT 59716
406 995-4644

Medicine Lake Outfitters
Tom Heintz
Box 3663, Bozeman, MT 59715
406 388-4938

Miller Outfitters
See **Elk Creek Outfitters**

Mountain Trail Outfitters
David B. Gamble
Rte. 38, Box 2249, Livingston
MT 59047   406 222-2734

Nine Quarter Circle Ranch
Kim and Kelly Kelsey
Gallatin Gateway, MT 59730
406 995-4276

Pintler Wilderness Outfitting
Bob & Dorothy Labert
Box 1116, Anaconda, MT 59711
406 563-7216

Rendezvous Outfitters
H. A. Moore
Box 447, Gardiner, MT 59030
406 848-7967

Gerald Richie & Son Outfitters
See Idaho

Rose Outfitters
Karen & John Rose
Box 508, Three Forks, MT 59752
406 285-6849

Rugg's Outfitting
See Idaho

Running M Outfitters
Monte & Martha McLane
Box 1282, Big Timber, MT 59011
406 932-6121

Rush's Lakeview Guest Ranch
2905 Harrison Ave, Butte, MT 59701
Win: 406 494-2585
Sum: 406 276-3300

Seven Lazy P Guest Ranch
Chuck and Sharon Blixrud
Box 178, Choteau, MT 59422
406 466-2044

S & W Outfitters
Sammy Smith
Box 228, Lewistown, MT 59457
406 538-5132

SG Outfitting
Steve Gamble
Box 221, Big Sky, MT 59716
406 995-4388

Selway-Magruder Outfitters
See Idaho

Simons Outfitters
See Idaho

Skyline Outfit[18]
Roland & Jane Cheek
Box 1880, Columbia Falls, MT 59912
406 892-5560

Sun River Outfitters
LLoyd and Carolyn Hahn
St. Rt. #2476, Condon, MT 59826
406 754-2228

Sweet Grass Ranch
Bill and Shelly Carroccia
Melville Route, Big Timber, MT 59011
Win: 406 537-4497 Sum: 406 537-4477

Trail Riders of the Wilderness
See District of Columbia

Triple Tree Ranch
Bill Myers
5520 Sourdough Rd, Bozeman
MT 59715   406 587-4821 406 587-8513

Wapiti Peak Outfitters
Ron & Jo Anne Carter
Box 423, White Sulphur Springs
MT 59645   406 547-2115

White Tail Ranch
Jack and Karen Hooker
Ovando, MT 59854   406 793-5666

Wilderness Lodge
See Hawkins Outfitters

Wild Country Outfitters
Don & Meg Merritt
713 Poplar, Helena, MT 59601
406 442-7127

---

[18]Combined horse pack trip and
white water rafting also available

Wilderness Country Outfitter
Frank & Gerri DeLeo
St. Rt. Box 423, Greenough, MT 59836
406 793-5702

Wilderness Outfitters
Smoke & Thelma Elser
3800 Rattlesnake Dr, Missoula
MT 59802   406 549-2820

Wildlife Outfitters & Guest Ranch
See Idaho

Ronnie L. Wright
Box 28, Roberts, MT 59070
or Box 1127 Cooke City, MT 59020
Oct -May: 406 445-2293
Jun-Sept: 406 838-2328

X Bar A Ranch
Boland Clark
McLeod, MT 59052   406 932-6108

63 Ranch
Mrs. Paul E. Christensen & Mrs. Sandra
  Cahill
Box 979, Livingston, MT 59047
406 222-0570

NEVADA

Breitenstein House
Lamoille, NV 89828   702 753-6356

Buckhorn Ranch
Box 219, Golconda, NV 89414
702 623-5374

Cottonwood Ranch
O'Neil Route, Wells, NV, 89835
702 752-3820   702 752-3604

Elko Guide Service
Bill Gibson and Pete Woolley
227 N. Belloak Ct., Elko, NV 89801
702 738-7539
Evenings: Dwayn Paskett 702 738-3403

Mountain View Guest Ranch
Starr Valley, Box 205, Wells, NV 89835
702 752-3772   702 752-3682

**Nevada High Country Outfitter and
  Guide Service**
Paul Bottari
Box 135, Wells, NV 89835
702 752-3809

Prunty Ranch
Frank Prunty
Charleston Route, Elko, NV 89801
Toll station Charleston 7882

NEW HAMPSHIRE

King's Western Trail Rides
Rt 3A, Hill, NH   603 934 5740

NEW MEXICO

American Wilderness Experience Inc
See Colorado

Jan Brown
Box 356, Regina, NM 87046
505 289-3394

East Fork Wilderness Ranch
Gary & Julie Webb
Rte 11, Box 75, Silver City, NM 88061
505 536-9368

Gila Hotsprings Vacation Center
HCR 88072, Gila Hotsprings
Silver City, NM 88061
505 536-9551

Dode Hershey
Box 1901, Santa Fe, NM 87501
505 471-6431

Quentin Hulse
Beaverhead Rte, Magdalena, NM 87825
505 772-5778

Mimbres Outfitters
Willard O. Fowler & Mark Miller
Box 47, Mimbres, NM 88049
505 536-9470

Michael Root
Box 35, Cuchillo, NM 87932
505 744-5919

San Francisco River Outfitters
Tom Klumker
Rt. 10, Box 179, Glenwood, NM 88039
505 539-2517

Sierra Grande Outfitters
Les Ezell
Box 321, Chama, NM 87520
505 756-2318

Trail Riders of the Wilderness
See District of Columbia

Trails West
Linda West
Mountain Route, Box 109
Jemez Springs, NM 87025
505 829-3787

Wilderness Ventures
Harley & Leah Jones
Box 393, Cliff, NM 88028
505 535-4118

NEW YORK

American Wilderness Experience Inc
See Colorado

Cold River Ranch
John Fontana
Rt. 3, Coreys, Tupper Lake, NY 12986
518 359-7559

Trail Riders of the Wilderness
See District of Columbia

NORTH CAROLINA

Cataloochee Ranch
Alice & Tom Aumen
Rt 1, Box 500, Maggie Valley, NC 28751
704 926-1401

Trail Riders of the Wilderness
See District of Columbia

NORTH DAKOTA

Long X Trail Ranch
Merv or Doreen Wike
Grassy Butte, ND 58634   701 842-2128

OHIO

Bear Creek Resort Ranch
3232 Downing St S.W., East Sparta
OH 44626   216 484-3901

Trail Riders of the Wilderness
See District of Columbia

OREGON

American Wilderness Experience Inc
See Colorado

Bennie Banks
DBA Wallowa Lake Corrals
Box 645, Joseph, OR 97846

Bar M Ranch
The Baker Family
Route 1, Box 263, Adams, OR 97810
503 566-3381

Cornucopia Wilderness Pack Station[19]
Eldon & Margaret Deardorff
Rt 1, Box 50, Richland, OR 97870
503 893-6400 Sum: 503 742-5400

Central Oregon Guide Service
61 Hackett Drive, Lapine, OR 97739
503 433-2753

Divide Wilderness Outfitters
Paul E. Brown
Box 49, Joseph, OR 97846
or 14 W. Jackson St., Medford
OR 97501   503 773-5983

Double Arrow Outfitters
Jack & C.B. Rich
Box 495, Seeley Lake, MT 59868
406 677-2317   406 677-2411

Eagle Gap Wilderness Pack Station[20]
Manford Isley
Rt. 1, Box 416, Joseph, OR 97846
503 432-4145

Flying M Ranch
Bryce and Barbara Mitchell and Family
23029 N.W, Flying M Road, Yamhill,
OR 97148   503 662-3222

Hell's Canyon Adventures, Inc.[20]
Gary & Bret Armacost
Box 159, Oxbow, OR 97840
503 785-3352   800 422-3568

High Cascade Stables & Pack Station
"A Division of Tic Cattle Co., Inc."
70775 Indian Ford Rd, Sisters, OR 97759
503 549-4972

High Country Outfitters, Inc[20]
Cal & Betsy Henry
Box 26, Joseph, OR 97846
503 432-9171

Lute Jerstad Adventures
Box 19537, Portland, OR 97219
503 224-4364

JP Pack Station
Jim &Betty Pyeatt
Box 101, Lostine, OR 97857
503 569-2204

Moss Springs Pack Station
Charlie and Peggy Short
Box 7, Union, OR 97883
503 562-5454

------
[19]Combined horse pack trip and
white water rafting also available

------
[20]Combined horse pack trip and
white water rafting also available

**Outback Ranch Outfitters and
   Outdoor Trip Consultants**
Ken, Tammie & Jon Wick
Box 384, Joseph, OR 97846
503 432-1721

Outdoor Adventures Plus
Larry Kirkpatrick
4030 West Amazon Dr, Eugene
OR 97405   503 344-4499

Pacific Crest Outward Bound School
0110 S.W. Bancroft, Portland, OR 97201
800 547-3312   503 243-1993

Quarter Circle Eleven Ranch
Marty Rust
990 West Main, Vale, OR 97918
208 362-5515

Ranch Recreational
Doug Muck
60775 Arnold Market, Bend, OR 97702
503 382-6259

Rocking Horse Ranch Inc.
28991 S.E. Hwy 224, Eagle Creek
OR 97022   503 637 3031

Sky Lakes Outfitters
Ron Goodpasture
372 Cheney Crk Rd, Grants Pass
OR 97527   503 476-3676

Steen's Wilderness Adventures[21]
Steens's Wild River Tours
Jim & Connie Steen
Box 216, Joseph, OR 97846
503 432-5315

---

[21]Combined horse pack trip and
white water rafting also available

Trail Riders of the Wilderness
See District of Columbia

Wapiti River Guides   See Idaho

SOUTH CAROLINA

Close Encounters
Box 100, Fort Mill, SC 29715
803 547-2644

SOUTH DAKOTA

Nemo Guest Ranch
Dale & June Deverman
Box 77, Nemo, SD 57759
605 578-2708

Smitty's Trail Rides
Deuane & Ann Smith
Win: Box 88, Hermosa, SD 57744
605 255- 4324
Sum: Box 162, Hill City, SD 57745
605 574-2084

TEXAS

Silver Spur Ranch
Mr. and Mrs. Tom Winchell
Box 1657, Bandera, TX 78003
512 796-3639

UTAH

Cache Valley Guide & Outfitters
437 West 200 South, Logan, UT 84321
801 752-7795

Canyon Rim Riders
Box 68, Orangeville, UT 84537
or Box 875, Castle Dale, UT 84513
801 748-2448   801 381-2496

Dammeron Valley Riding Stables, Inc
Box 193, Ivins, UT 84738 801 628-6677

**Eagle Basin Outfitting & Guide
   Service, Inc**
Box 947, Parowan, UT 84761
801 477-8837

Ed Black Horse Tours
Box 155, Mexican Hat, UT 84531
801 739-4285 801 727-3287 message at
   Monument Valley info center

Hondoo Rivers & Trails
Box 306, Torrey, UT 84775
801 425-3519

Honeymoon Trail Company
General Delivery, Moccasin, AZ 86022
602 643-7292

Horsehead Pack Trips
Box 68, Monticello, UT 84535
801 587-2929

Ken Slight Pack Trips
Box 1270, Moab, UT 84532
801 259-5505

Outlaw Trails
Box 129, Hanksville, UT 84738
801 542-3221   801 542-3421

Outlaw Trails, Inc
Box 336, Green River, UT 84525
801 564-3477

Pack Creek Ranch
Ken & Jane Sleight
Box 1270, Moab, UT 84532

Pine Valley Pack Trips
41 West 300 South, LaVerkin, UT 84745
801 635-2602

Piute Creek Outfitters Inc.
Barbara & Arch Arnold
Ranch Rte. 1, Kamas, UT 84036
801 783-4317   801 486-2607
800 225-0218

Rick Marchal Pack Trips
Box 918, Hurricane, UT 84737
801 635-4950

Ruby Ranch[22]
Green River, UT 84525
801 564-3538

Terry Albrecht Horse Pack Trips
Box 202, Hanksville, UT 84734
801 542-3216

Trail Riders of the Wilderness
See District of Columbia

WASHINGTON

Back Country Outfitters
6806 Interurban Blvd, Snohomish
WA 98290   206 668-6437

Cascade Corrals
Stehekin Valley Ranch
Box 36, Stehikin, WA 98852
509 682-4677

Cascade Wilderness & Wildlife Outfitters
Box 172, Twisp, WA 98856
509 997-0155   509 997-7492

Crystal Mountain Corral
Crystal Mountain, WA 98022
206 663-2340

Eagle Creek Ranch
Box 719, Leavenworth, WA 98826
509 548-7798

Early Winters Outfitters
c/o Aaron L Burkhart
Mazama, WA 98833
509 996-2659   509 996-2355

Flying Eagle Outfitters
Box 528, Packwood, WA 98361
206 494-9249

Bill Hansen Saddle and Pack Horses
Box 13, Malaga, WA 98828
509 662-2474

Happy Trails Horseback Riding Ranch
10719 - 142nd Place S. E., Renton
WA 98056   206 226-7848

High Country Packers
Box 108, Issaquah, WA 98027
206 392-0111   206 392-5403

Hidden River Ranch
Route 3, Box 1082, Hoquiam, WA 98550
206 533-2096

Icicle Outfitters & Guides, Inc
Box 322, Leavenworth, WA 98826
509 784-1145   509 763-3647

Indian Creek Corral
Star Route, Box 218, Naches, WA 98937
509 925-2062

Gerhard Jorgenson
Box 757, Issaquah, WA 98027
206 788-5103

Lawson Livestock Co
1341 W. Valley Road, Friday Harbor
WA 98250   206 378-4313

Claude Miller
Winthrop, WA 98862   509 996-2350

Lost Mountain Ranch
Box 562, Sequim, WA 98382
206 683-4331

Morgan's Pack Trips
2901 S. Skagit Hwy
Sedro Woolley, WA 98284
206 826-4375 Sum: 509 658-2433

North Cascade Outfitters
Box 397, Brewster, WA 98812
Weekdays: 509 689-2813
Weekends and evenings: 509 996-2010

North Cascade Safari
Box 250, Winthrop, WA 98862
509 966-2350

Ole's Cascade Packers
Star Route, Box 15, Twisp, WA 98856
509 997-5844

---

[22]Combined horse pack trip and
white water rafting also available

Olympic Adventures
Star Route 1, Box 662, Forks, WA 98331
206 374-6784

Outback Ranch Outfitters
See Oregon

Rock'n H Packers
Box 294, Quincy, WA 98848
509 785-3333

Sandene's Horse Trail Rides
13021 N.E. 100th Street, Kirkland
WA 98033   206 822-1805

St. Joe Hunting & Fishing Camp Inc
See Idaho

Sun Sparks Ranches
7832 N.E. 146th, Bothell, WA 98011
206 663-2575

Susee's Skyline Packers
1807 East 72nd Street, Tacoma
WA 98404   206 472-5558

Ted Thorndike Ranch
Rt 1, Box 72, Oroville, WA 98844
509 476-3777

Trail Riders of the Wilderness
See District of Columbia

White Eagle Visions Expeditions
401 Ekone Ranch Road, Goldendale
WA 98620   509 773-4026

WEST VIRGINIA

Back Forty Stables
McHarris Inn, US 19, Mt. Nebo
WV 26679   304 872-5151

Circle H and Tranquil Meadows
Rt 1, Box 330, Bruceton Mills
WV 26525   304 379-4808   304 379-3875

Coolfont Re+Creation Stables
Rt 9 W, Berkeley Springs, WV 25411
304 258-4500

Lost River State Park Stables
Rt 2, Box 24, Mathias, WV 26812
304 897-5372   1 800 CALL WVA

Pipestem Resort State Park Stable
Rt 20, Pipestem, WV 25979
304 466-1800   1 800 CALL WVA

Red Creek Quarter Horse Stables, Inc
Star Rt, Box 50, Dry Fork, WV 26263
304 866-4728

Watoga State Park Jadalee Stables
Star Rt l, Box 252, Marlington
WV 24954
304 799-4087 1 800 CALL WVA

WISCONSIN

Whitecap Mountain Resort
Hwy E, Box E, Montreal, WI 54550
715 561-2227   715 561-2776

Wilderness Pursuit
Rt 3, Box 169, Niellsville, WI 54456
715 743-4484

WYOMING

Absaroka Mountain Lodge
Box 168, Wapiti, WY 82450
307 587-3963

Absaroka Ranch
Budd and Emi Betts
Star Route, Dubois, WY 82513
307 455-2275

**Allen Brothers Wilderness Ranch &
  Outfitting**[23]
Phil & Jim Allen
Box 243, Lander, WY 82520
307 332-2995   307 332-5519

American Wilderness Experience Inc
See Colorado

Big Sandy Lodge
Bernie and Connie Kelly
Box 223, Boulder, WY 82923

Bitterroot Ranch
See **Equitour**

Blackwater Lodge
Chris and Jane LaBuy
1516 North Fork Hwy, Cody, WY 82414
307 587-3709

Boulder Lake Lodge
Box 1100, Pinedale, WY 82941
307 367-2961

Box K Ranch
Walt Korn
Moran, WY 83013   307 543-2407

Box R Ranch
Irv Lozier
Cora, WY 82925   307 367-2291

Bridger Wilderness Outfitters
Tim Singewald
Box 561, Pinedale, WY 82941
307 367-2268

[23]Packing school also available

Cabin Creek Outfitters
Duane & Betsy Wiltse
1313 Lane 10, Rt 1, Powell, WY 82435
307 754-9279

Castle Rock Ranch
Joe and Allison Tilden
412 Rd. 6NS, Cody, WY 82414.
307 527-7159   307 587-2076

Cross Mill Iron Ranch
Mr. and Mrs. Larry Miller
Crowheart, WY 82512   307 486-2279

Crossed Sabres Ranch
Fred and Alvie Norris
Wapiti, WY 82450   307 587-3750

Darwin Ranch
Box 511, Jackson, WY 83001
307 733-5588

David Ranch
Daniel, WY 83115   307 859-8228

Deer Haven Lodge
Bill and Stella Hughes
Bill & June Littlefield
Box 76, Ten Sleep, WY 82442
307 366-2449

Diamond D Ranch and Outfitters
Box 211, Moran, WY 83013
307 543-2479

Double Bar J Ranch
Larry Stetter
Box 695, Dubois, WY 82513
307 455-2725

Eaton's Ranch
Wolf, WY 82844
307 655-9285   307 655-9552

Elk Track Ranch
Kennis and Marsha Lutz
Box 53, Kelly, WY 83011
307 733-6171

Equitour
Bayard & Mel Fox & Billie Finley
Bitterroot Ranch
East Fork, Rt 66, Box 1042, Dubois
WY 82513
800 545-0019   307 455-2778
Telex WUI 6502408901

L. D. Frome, Outfitter[24]
Box G, Afton, WY 83110
307 886-5240

Game Hill Ranch
Pete & Holly Cameron
Box A, Bondurant, WY 82922
307 733-4120

Goff Creek Lodge
Gloria T Schmitt
Box 155, Cody, WY 82414
307 587-3753

Goosewing Ranch
Bill and Phyllis Clark
Box 70, Kelly, WY 83011   307 733-2768

Green River Guest Ranch
Box 32, Cora, WY 82925   307 367-2314

Grizzly Ranch
Rick and Candy Felts
North Fork, Route A, Cody, WY 82414
307 587-3966

Heart Six Ranch
Cameron & Billie Garnick
Box 70, Moran, Jackson Hole
WY 83013   307 543-2477   307 733-6994

Hidden Valley Ranch
Duane and Sheila Hagen
Tony and Lin Scheiber
153 Hidden Valley Rd, Cody, WY 82414
307 587-5090

Jackson Hole Trail Rides[25]
Walt Korn
Box 110, Moran, WY 83013
307 543-2407

**Kamp Dakota Campground and Guest
  Ranch**
Box 595, Wheatland, WY 82201
307 322-2772

Lazy L and B Ranch
Barnard and Leota Didier
Dubois, WY 82513
Wanda S. Smith
Box 95, Moose, WY 83012
307 733-3435

Monk's Summer Camp
Charles N. Monk
Box 12 R.F.D., Lovell, WY 82431
307 548-6686

Moore Guest Ranch
Box 293, Encampment, WY 82325
307 327-5574

**Mountain Shadows Guest Ranch and
  UXU Lodge**
Box 110, Wapiti, WY 82450
307 587-2143

---

[24]Horse trekking

[25]Horse trekking

Paradise Guest Ranch
Jim and Leah Anderson
Box 790, Buffalo, WY 82834
307 684-7876   307 684-5254

Pellatz Ranch
Don and Betty Pellatz
1031 Steinle Rd, Rt 2, Douglas
WY 82633   307 358-2380

Pines Lodge
Box 100, Buffalo, WY 82834

R Lazy S Ranch
Claire C. McGonaughy
Win: 2479 Holiday Ranch Loop Rd
Park City, UT 84060   801 649-8086
Sum: Box 308, Teton Village, WY 83025
307 733-2633

Ralph Miller's Wilderness Pack Trips
Cooke City, MO 59020

Red Rock Ranch
Box 38, Kelly, WY 83011
307 733-6288   Win: 307 755-2225

Rimrock Dude Ranch
Glenn and Alice Fales
2728 Northfork Hwy, Cody, WY 82414
307 587-3970   307 587-3747

Schively Ranch
Joe and Iris Bassett
1062 Road 15, Lovell, WY 82431
307 548-6688

Seven D Ranch
Marshall Dominick
Box 100, Cody, WY 82414
Win: 307 587-9885   Sum: 307 587-3997

Shoshone Lodge
Box 790, Cody, WY 82414
307 587-4044

Siggins Triangle X Ranch
Stan and Lila Siggins
3453 Southfork Road, Cody, WY 82414
307 587-2031

**Skinner Brothers Guides and
   Outfitters**
Robert Skinner
Box 859, Pinedale, WY 82941
307 367-4675

Spring Creek Ranch
Steve and Dallas Robertson
Box 1033, Bondurant, WY 82922
307 733-3974

Sweetwater Gap Ranch
Box 26, Rock Springs, WY 82901
307 362-2798

Teton Expeditions, Inc
See Idaho

Thorofare Outfitting
Donald C. Schmalz
Red Pole Ranch, Wapiti, WY 82450
307 587-5929

Togwotee Mountain Lodge
Dave & Judie Helgeson
Box 91, Moran, WY 83013
307 543-2847

Trail Creek Ranch
Elizabeth Woolsey
Wilson, WY 83014   307 733-2610

Trail Riders of the Wilderness
See District of Columbia

Trails End Ranch
Box 20311, Jackson, WY 83001
307 733-1616

Triangle X Ranch
Box 120, Moose, WY 83012
307 733-2183   307 733-5500

Turpin Meadow Ranch
Box 48, Moran, WY 83013
307 543-2496   307 733-6521

Two Bar Spear Ranch
Grant & Abigail Beck
Box 251, Pinedale, WY 82941
307 367-4637
Nov-May: Box 86, Florence, MO 65329
816 368-2801

Two Bars Seven Ranch
Box 67, Tie Siding, WY 82084
307 742-6072   307 745-5049

Valley Ranch
Valley Ranch Road W, Cody, WY 82414

White Pine Lodge
Box 833, Pinedale, WY 82941
307 367-4121

4-Bear Outfitters
1297 Ln 10, Rt 1, Powell, WY 82435

7-D Ranch
Box 100, Cody, WY 82414
307 587-9885   307 587-3997

Notes:

Bibliography

Horses, Hitches & Rocky Trails "The Packers Bible", Joe Black
Johnson Books, Boulder, Colorado, U.S.A.

In the Saddle A Basic Guide to Riding, Manfred W. Meyer
The Hayes Publishing Group of Sparkford, Yeovil, Somerset, England

Keeping Warm and Dry, Harry Roberts
Stonewall Press, Washington, D.C., U.S.A.

Know all About Tack, George Dulaney
Farnam Horse Library, Omaha, Nebraska, U.S.A.

The New Horse Owner's Illustrated Manual, Guy Perrault
Editions Grand Prix Reg'd, St. Isidore de Dorchester, P.Q., Canada

Photography & the Art of Seeing, Freeman Patterson
Van Nostrand Reinhold Ltd., Toronto, Ontario, Canada and New York, N.Y., U.S.A.

Photography for the Joy of It, Freeman Patterson
Van Nostrand Reinhold Ltd., Toronto, Ontario, Canada and New York, N.Y., U.S.A.

Photography of Natural Things, Freeman Patterson
Van Nostrand Reinhold, Toronto, Ontario, Canada and New York, N.Y., U.S.A.

A Place to Start Learning to Handle Your Horse, Sylvia Brooks
Arco Publishing Co. Inc., New York, N.Y., U.S.A.

Practical Western Training, Dave Jones
Arco Publishing Co. Inc., New York, N.Y., U.S.A.

The Rider's Handbook A step-by-step course, Sally Gordon
Chartwell Books Inc., Secaucus, New Jersey, U.S.A.

There are No Problem Horses only Problem Riders, Mary Twelveponies
Houghton Mifflin Co., Boston, Mass., U.S.A.

Western Horsemanship, Richard Shrake
The Western Horseman Inc., Colorado Springs, Colorado, U.S.A.

INDEX

About the Author

Helen James was born in London, England in 1929. Her father, Col. A.E. Powell, retired from the British Army, brought the family to North America in 1934 and for the next ten years travelled with them through forty-seven of the United States, nine Canadian provinces, Hawaii and Mexico. Helen settled in Metropolitan Toronto with her husband, Arthur, and since her five children have left home has returned to the Rocky Mountains most summers to trail ride.

While her children were growing up Helen obtained her Bachelor of Arts degree from the University of Toronto.
Her interest in photography started in 1975 when she bought her husband a single-lens-reflex camera for his birthday.
She is a life member of the Trail Riders of the Canadian Rockies, and past-president of the Seven Oaks Camera Club and the Scarborough Cross Country Ski Club. Other interests include paddling and building canoes.

Outfitter's Information Form

If you are an outfitter who provides horse pack trips please fill in this form to ensure accurate listing in the next edition of this book. Type or print clearly, enclose two brochures and send to Plas y Bryn Press, Box 97, West Hill, Ontario M1E 4R4, Canada.

Name of organization..

Name of contact person...

Address..

....

....Phone number.........................

Do you offer horse pack trips for non-hunters	yes	no
Do you offer horse pack trips for hunters	yes	no
Do you offer combined horse pack and float trips?	yes	no
Do you offer a packing or guiding school?	yes	no

Date...Signature...

Photocopy this form if needed.

Book Order Form

Please send me .... copies of *Trail Riding: The Wilderness from Horseback*

      Hardcover at $24.95 in Canadian funds or $20.95 in U.S. funds
      Softcover at $18.95 in Canadian funds or $15.95 in U.S. funds $............

              add $2.00 postage and shipping   2.00
                                                        ————

              Enclose cheque or money order for $............

Name..

Address..

....Postal or Zip Code........................

Mail to: Plas y Bryn Press
                Box 97, West Hill, Ontario
                M1E 4R4, Canada

Cut here --

Book Order Form

Please send me .... copies of *Trail Riding: The Wilderness from Horseback*

      Hardcover at $24.95 in Canadian funds or $20.95 in U.S. funds
      Softcover at $18.95 in Canadian funds or $15.95 in U.S. funds $............

              add $2.00 postage and shipping   2.00
                                                           ————

              Enclose cheque or money order for $............

Name..

Address..

....Postal or Zip Code........................

Mail to: Plas y Bryn Press
                Box 97, West Hill, Ontario
                M1E 4R4, Canada